HOUSE

European Union Committee

5th Report of Session 2007–08

The Single Market: Wallflower or Dancing Partner?

Inquiry into the European Commission's Review of the Single Market

Volume I: Report

Ordered to be printed 31 January 2008 and published 8 February 2008

Published by the Authority of the House of Lords

London : The Stationery Office Limited
£11.00

HL Paper 36-I

The European Union Committee

The European Union Committee is appointed by the House of Lords "to consider European Union documents and other matters relating to the European Union". The Committee has seven Sub-Committees which are:

Economic and Financial Affairs, and International Trade (Sub-Committee A)
Internal Market (Sub-Committee B)
Foreign Affairs, Defence and Development Policy (Sub-Committee C)
Environment and Agriculture (Sub-Committee D)
Law and Institutions (Sub-Committee E)
Home Affairs (Sub-Committee F)
Social and Consumer Affairs (Sub-Committee G)

Our Membership

The Members of the European Union Committee are:

Lord Blackwell
Baroness Cohen of Pimlico
Lord Dykes
Lord Freeman
Lord Grenfell (Chairman)
Lord Harrison
Baroness Howarth of Breckland
Lord Jopling
Lord Kerr of Kinlochard
Lord Maclennan of Rogart
Lord Mance
Lord Plumb
Lord Powell of Bayswater
Lord Roper
Lord Sewel
Baroness Symons of Vernham Dean
Lord Tomlinson
Lord Wade of Chorlton
Lord Wright of Richmond

The Members of the Sub-Committee which carried out this inquiry (Sub-Committee B: Internal Market) are:

Lord Bradshaw
Lord Dykes
Baroness Eccles of Moulton*
Lord Freeman (Chairman)
Lord Fyfe of Fairfield*
Lord Geddes*
Lord Haskel*
Lord James of Blackheath
Lord Lee of Trafford*
Lord Mitchell
Lord Paul
Lord Powell of Bayswater
Lord Rowe-Beddoe
Lord St John of Bletso*
Lord Walpole
Lord Whitty

*Former Members from the last session (2006–07), co-opted to complete the inquiry.

Information about the Committee

The reports and evidence of the Committee are published by and available from The Stationery Office. For information freely available on the web, our homepage is:
http://www.parliament.uk/parliamentary_committees/lords_eu_select_committee.cfm
There you will find many of our publications, along with press notices, details of membership and forthcoming meetings, and other information about the ongoing work of the Committee and its Sub-Committees, each of which has its own homepage.

General Information

General information about the House of Lords and its Committees, including guidance to witnesses, details of current inquiries and forthcoming meetings is on the internet at
http://www.parliament.uk/about_lords/about_lords.cfm

Contacts for the European Union Committee

Contact details for individual Sub-Committees are given on the website.
General correspondence should be addressed to the Clerk of the European Union Committee, Committee Office, House of Lords, London, SW1A 0PW
The telephone number for general enquiries is 020 7219 6225.
The Committee's email address is euclords@parliament.uk

CONTENTS

NOTE: References in the text of the report are as follows:
(Q) refers to a question in oral evidence
(p) refers to a page of written evidence

The Report of the Committee is published in Volume I, HL Paper No 36-I
The Evidence of the Committee is published in Volume II, HL Paper No 36-II

FOREWORD—What this Report is about

This report is about the need for the Commission and Member States to take action in order to prevent the Single Market project from failing to achieve expectations. Often referred to as one of the greatest achievements of the European Union, it must not be allowed to slip into decline by the failure of Member States to live up to their commitments and make the Single Market a reality for all.

Achieving the completion of the Single Market is fundamental to reviving support for the European Union: in order to create, as Commission President Barroso has said, "a Europe of results", action needs to be taken now.

Policy-making and Implementation

Increased competition, lower prices and a wider choice of products and services are the potential benefits to consumers; access to an enormous home market is the potential benefit to business. In reality the failure of Member States to implement important legislation has maintained barriers and prevented the fuller completion of the Single Market. This failure is aggravated by the growing trend towards economic protectionism in a number of Member States. Misguided attempts to protect domestic industries and safeguard national jobs are preventing consumers and businesses from reaping the full benefits of a truly open Single Market.

In order to move the Single Market project forward the EU needs to reassess the tools it uses. The legislative route is not always the most effective means for achieving Single Market goals. The increased use of other, non-legislative tools will help to overcome the difficulties of legislating for an expanded EU.

We believe that achieving consistent implementation begins with effective policy-making based on detailed sector-specific understanding. In addition to better consultation upstream in the legislative process the Commission has a role to play earlier in the implementation process as a facilitator and enabler. More resources should be devoted to providing practical assistance to Member States in the process of transposing legislation in order to avoid problems of interpretation, delayed implementation or failure to enforce later on.

The focus on assisting Member States early on in the process of transposition must not come at the expense of effective enforcement when necessary.

Regulatory Authorities

National Regulatory Authorities (NRAs) must be independent of government, especially where governments have financial interests in the major market operator or national incumbent. This is essential to generate consumer and market confidence, and is the best way to ensure a fair application of the rules.

There is no need for a 'super-regulator' at EU-level in any of the sectors we considered in this inquiry, which were energy, telecommunications and financial services. However, there is a need for greater and better coordination between NRAs, especially in matters regarding the cross-border provision of services. This is essential if market access is to become a reality—especially for consumers and SMEs.

Realising the Benefits for Businesses, Citizens and Consumers

Very few SMEs are engaged in cross-border activity and this is largely due to the regulatory barriers which remain in place, and the lack of reliable information to assist businesses. The Commission has made the objective of engaging small business in the Single Market the centre-piece of its Review and we welcome and support this aim.

We conclude that values and social benefits are as important to reconnect Europe with its citizens as are economic advantages. The Commission must ensure that clear and accessible information is available about social, as well as economic, benefits.

We are concerned by evidence of support for "national champions" in some Member States. Such practices are contrary to the principles of the Single Market and will not benefit consumers or businesses. We call for a renewed commitment to the importance of free and undistorted competition and the need to complete the Single Market for the benefit of consumers and businesses alike.

Energy

Having considered the evidence, we are of the opinion that full ownership unbundling in the energy sector more satisfactorily removes the incentives for discriminatory and uncompetitive behaviour by network operators. We note the argument that security of supply is important but we are not convinced that the creation of a more comprehensive Single Market in energy would necessarily weaken international supply.

Telecommunications

The Committee supports the Commission's proposal to enable NRAs to impose functional separation as a remedy to reduce further the market power of the national incumbents. Functional separation is where an operator places the provision of certain wholesale access products in an independently operated business unit supplying all market players on equal terms and conditions, including the operator's own retail business.

Financial Services

We believe that there should be a pause in the regulation of the wholesale banking sector so that the impact of existing measures can be assessed and implementation can be encouraged. It is important for any initiatives in the retail banking sector to have a consumer-oriented approach and should be based on research and consultation. Following such research and consultation the Commission should be more willing to develop a combination of market-led and regulatory instruments.

Inquiry into the European Commission's Review of the Single Market

CHAPTER 1: INTRODUCTION

1. In May 2006 the Commission launched its review of the Single Market[1]. Following hard on the heels of recent set-backs—the failure of France and the Netherlands to ratify the European Constitution—the review was an attempt to reinvigorate the Single Market as a means of creating jobs in the European Union, and thus recapture popular support for the European project. The Commission argued that it needed to reconnect with Europe's citizens, to remind them of the benefits of being in the European Union, and to reassure them that their needs were at the heart of the project. An open and fully functioning Single Market was considered a key policy plank in meeting these objectives.

2. In launching the review, the Commission freely acknowledged that the four freedoms (the free movement of goods, services, persons and capital) were not yet a reality. The Commission set out to answer the following key questions: how can we build on what has already been achieved? Where are the remaining gaps? How can we meet the challenges of the future? Do we have the most effective mechanisms for delivering the Single Market?

3. This Committee launched its inquiry into the Commission's review of the Single Market in May 2007. In order to restrict the scope of the inquiry to a manageable size, we have largely focused on three specific sectors—energy, telecommunications and financial services—as well as taking evidence on the wider issues affecting the Single Market. This report will highlight the common themes which have emerged across the three sectors, and reflect on lessons for the Single Market as a whole. There are a number of other issues which have an impact on the functioning of the Single Market, each of which carries the risk of distorting free competition. These include the use of state financial assistance, common employment or insolvency laws, growing cross-border internet trade and the protection of EU patents. It is not within the scope of this report to address these. The Committee intends to return to these issues.

4. The Committee heard oral evidence from a wide range of witnesses, and received a large volume of written submissions. The Committee travelled to Brussels on two occasions to meet with further witnesses. Witnesses are listed in Appendix 2 and we are grateful to them all. We also thank our Special Advisers Dean Cook, Mark Griffiths, and Dr Ian Walden.

5. We have reported after the publication of the Commission's review[2] intentionally in order to offer our own comments on their conclusions, and to help inform discussion at the Spring European Council 2008, when further

---

1 A Citizens Agenda; delivering results for Europe, COM (2006) 211 final.

2 A Single Market for the 21st Century, COM (2007) 724 final, 20 November 2007.

proposals are expected. However, we believe that this subject will continue to be highly relevant for many years. The Single Market has the potential to be of the widest significance for consumers and businesses alike, and reaching its full potential will take time and commitment; we hope that our conclusions will make a contribution to that effort.

6. We make this report to the House for debate.

CHAPTER 2: THE SINGLE MARKET

Origins: Treaty of Rome 1957

7. The Single Market became a reality in January 1993, establishing the principles of free movement of goods, people, services and capital.

8. The idea behind the Single Market was presaged in the Treaty of Rome, which established the European Economic Community (EEC) in 1957. It enshrined the objective of increasing economic prosperity by creating a common market through the elimination of trade barriers between Member States. The aim was to liberalise exchanges of goods and services by removing customs duties within the EEC, establishing a common external tariff, and eliminating quantitative restrictions (import quotas) and measures of equivalent effect. The completely free movement of goods was to be accompanied by the free movement of persons (especially employed persons), services and, to a certain extent, capital.

9. The customs union was achieved by 1 July 1968. It saw the abolition of internal tariff barriers and quotas. Progress was also made towards the free movement of workers: for the first time a citizen was able to take up employment in another Member State and enjoy the same conditions as citizens of the host country. A degree of tax harmonisation was established with the introduction of VAT in 1970.

10. Progress in reducing barriers in other areas however was less rapid and the free movement of goods and services continued to be hampered by so-called "non-tariff barriers" such as national technical rules governing products. Furthermore, while service-providers could no longer be discriminated against on the grounds of nationality, in practice they were required to comply with a wide range of national regulations which varied from one Member State to another. Anti-competitive practices, such as exclusive production, service rights or the use of state aids, continued. All these barriers constituted the maintenance of the concept of internal frontiers; this was a common market only in name.

11. The failure to complete the common market was seen as having a significant economic cost, "the cost of non-Europe" as it was described at the time. This failure was largely attributed to the decision to using detailed legislative harmonisation to remove the remaining non-tariff barriers; reaching agreement on such legislation was extremely difficult as it required Council decisions, most of which had to be taken by unanimity.

Re-launch: Single European Act 1986

12. The slowing down of the common market project was symptomatic of the stagnation affecting European integration in the late 1970s and early 1980s. What was described by academics and commentators as 'euro-sclerosis' took hold of the European Economic Community. This state of sclerosis led many in the Community to look for a way to reignite the project.

13. The re-invigoration of the European project was to be achieved by the rejuvenation of one of the core ideas behind the Rome Treaty, the total removal of the frontier concept to create an area where human and material resources could move freely. Member States gave their approval to the aim of

creating a fully-fledged internal market at the European Council in March 1985, with the UK taking a leading role in the discussions. It was agreed to set the end of 1992 as the completion date, and the Commission was asked to prepare a programme and timetable for implementation.

14. The commitment to creating the internal market was enshrined in the Single European Act, which was signed in February 1986. The Act had two objectives: first, the inclusion in the Treaty of the concept of the internal market, setting a deadline for its completion; second, giving the Council effective decision-making machinery by introducing qualified majority voting, and thereby removing the requirement for unanimity, which had hitherto hindered the adoption and implementation of necessary legislation. This streamlining of the decision-making process enabled the Community to move passed the bottleneck of arguments about harmonisation or mutual recognition of legislation and make progress in completing the Single Market.

15. The underlying desire was to re-invigorate the European project by creating "opportunities for growth, for job creation, for economies of scale, for improved productivity and profitability, for healthier competition, for professional and business mobility, for stable prices and for consumer choice"[3]. The UK was an enthusiastic supporter of that process.

16. Despite not all the necessary legislation being in place, the Single Market was formally launched on 1 January 1993.

Responsibility for the Single Market

17. In examining the Single Market the Committee found it helpful to distinguish between the roles of different institutions. The Single Market is a shared endeavour between the European Institutions, the Member States, the National Regulatory Authorities, and the European Court of Justice.

The European Institutions

18. The Commission is responsible for drafting legislation. Approval is then required by the Council and, in many cases, the European Parliament. Where approval is needed under the co-decision procedure the Council and European Parliament must reach an agreement or compromise before legislation can be enacted.

19. As guardian of the Treaties the Commission has an important role in monitoring the timely transposition and implementation of legislation by Member States. The Commission monitors this with its bi-annual Internal Market Scoreboard, which tracks the deficit between the number of internal market laws adopted at EU level and those adopted in Member States. The Commission is empowered to initiate infringement proceedings against Member States who fail to comply with Single Market rules (see paragraph 22 below).

The Member States

20. The role of Member States is two-fold: they make up the Council which influences the Commission's legislative agenda, and subsequently agree

---

[3] Foreword by Commissioner Lord Cockfield, Cecchini Report, 1988

proposed legislation; following agreement it is Member States who are responsible for implementing the legislation.

The National Regulatory Authorities

21. National Regulatory Authorities (NRAs) are responsible for applying the rules that have been transposed by Member States. NRAs have been set up in each Member State for each of the sectors under examination in this inquiry—energy, telecommunications and financial services.

The European Court of Justice

22. An intransient Member State can be brought before the European Court of Justice. Under Article 226 of the EC Treaty the Commission can initiate infringement proceedings against Member States on the basis of non-compliance of national implementing measures, or incorrect application of directives. A ruling from the European Court of Justice takes on average 20 months from the commencement of proceedings. In 2006 103 infringements were declared against Member States.

CHAPTER 3: THE SINGLE MARKET TODAY

The Impact of the Single Market so far

23. Two decades after the adoption of the Single European Act, and 14 years after the launch of the Single Market, the majority of the evidence received by the Committee suggests that its impact, so far, has been positive. It has facilitated the creation of a home market of 500 million consumers, making the EU the world's largest trading bloc, and "a very attractive investment location" with a strong position in the global economy (Harbour, Purvis, Wilcox p 221).

24. According to the Commission the estimated gains from the Single Market amount to 2.2% of EU growth and 1.4% of total employment (or 2.75 million jobs) over the period 1992–2006 (p 86). In its response to the Commission's review the Government suggested that the Single Market had boosted prosperity in the EU by 1.8% GDP or €225 billion in 2006 alone[4]. Business for New Europe submitted evidence that the European Single Market had the largest GDP of any economy in the world, accounting for 40% of global trade (p 204).

25. The Government argued that the Single Market had boosted competition and led to a reduction in prices, pointing to the convergence in product prices in the late 1990s as evidence of increased competitiveness[5].

26. Business for New Europe estimated that the Single Market is worth £20 billion annually to the UK: around 50% of the UK's trade is with the rest of Europe, and approximately 3 million jobs are linked to EU exports (p 205). The Single Market has also sparked large increases in foreign direct investment, much of which has benefited the UK (p 204).

27. Another significant benefit of the Single Market has been the improved ease of movement across borders, for students, workers, holiday-makers and pensioners. According to Commission data, 1.2 million students across Europe have completed part of their studies in another Member State; and 15 million Europeans have moved across borders to work or retire (Q 199). According to a Eurobarometer survey, three-quarters of EU citizens find travelling abroad much easier today (Q 199)—a finding which is supported by the fact that British people alone made 53 million visits to the rest of Europe in 2006, an increase of 50% since 1998 (Business for New Europe p 206). It is also estimated that over a million Britons live, work and study in other EU Member States, whilst since 2004 around 600,000 people from the accession countries have come to the UK (Business for New Europe p 206).

28. There have been other benefits to consumers—Commission surveys suggest that 73% of EU citizens consider access to a wider choice of high quality goods and services one of the major benefits of the Single Market; 67% of citizens welcome the increase in competition in areas like transport, communications and financial services brought about by the Single Market; and 53% of European consumers consider that Single Market regulation has increased consumer protection within the EU (Q 199). Single Market

---

4 The Single Market: A Vision for the 21st Century, HMT & DTI, January 2007

5 *Ibid.*

regulations have in general set high standards for the protection of the consumer, the environment, health and other standards that are, in some cases, applied in other regions of the world (Q 275).

Enlargement

29. The Single Market today is a very different undertaking to the Single Market of 1993 and this is chiefly due to successive waves of enlargement. This Committee has been a strong supporter of the enlargement process and we recognised the positive economic and political impact which it has had on the European Union in our recent report *The Further Enlargement of the EU: threat or opportunity?* (53rd report, 2005–06, HL 273).

30. Enlargement has had a profound impact on the Single Market. According to the Government, the 2004 and 2007 enlargements have increased the size of the Single Market by 104 million consumers, and the EU GDP was around €850 billion larger in 2007 than it would otherwise have been (p 143). Investment opportunities have increased and this is reflected in the sharp increase in UK trade with the eight central and eastern European countries that joined in 2004: £6.4 billion in 2005, up 151% since 1995; UK trade with Romania and Bulgaria was just over £1 billion, up 250% over the same period (HM Treasury p 143). Lord Williamson of Horton, former Secretary-General of the European Commission, agreed that the growth potential of the new Member States was a very important element of the enlarged Single Market (Q 17).

31. Inevitably however, "the increased divergence among the 27 Member States constitutes a challenge to [the Single Market's] proper functioning" (Commission p 86) and this was recognised by many witnesses: most importantly, agreement of legislation, transposition and implementation have become much more difficult in an enlarged EU. BusinessEurope, the European employers' organisation, stressed how much more difficult implementation of Single Market regulation has become in the enlarged EU, and made a range of proposals for its improvement, including the training of national officials and judges, and the improvement of non-judicial resolution mechanisms such as arbitration or mediation in cases of disputes (Q 275). We consider the issue of legislation and implementation in greater detail below.

32. Enlargement has also had a significant impact on the movement of labour. Our inquiry did not consider this in detail.

Legislation and the Single Market

33. With enlargement the task of transposition and implementation of the Single Market rules has become much more complex. The latest issue of the Internal Market Scoreboard provides data to support this. The average transposition deficit recorded in July 2007 was 1.6% (or 1.8% if Romania and Bulgaria are included). However, the percentages do not immediately reflect the magnitude of the problem—the Internal Market *acquis* is made up of 1628 directives and 679 regulations[6]; Portugal with a deficit of 4.4% has failed to implement 71 internal market directives; in Italy it is 44 directives,

---

6 As at 30 April 2007. The "*acquis*" means the body of Community laws in force.

in the Czech Republic 38 and in Poland 29[7]. The UK, despite being within the target 1.5% deficit, has failed to transpose 19 directives. The effect of the non-application of these rules is difficult to quantify, but clearly the failure to transpose directives does not help the further development of the Single Market.

34. The failure of Member States to implement fully existing legislation was a recurring theme throughout the evidence received, especially in the energy and telecoms sectors. Indeed, many witnesses commented that the sectors under consideration were not so much in need of reform as in need of having existing legislation evenly applied across the Member States (see paragraphs 84–85, 109–110 and 130).

35. There is also a qualitative element to the transposition and implementation of legislation which is evidenced by the number of infringement proceedings for the incorrect transposition or application of directives, which continues to rise[8]. It was argued by Dr Mark Thatcher, of the London School of Economics Public Policy Group, that the nature of legislation emanating from Brussels—described as "incredibly broad ... a set of objectives with very little detail" (Q 29)—allowed for significant differences in interpretation during transposition into national law. This was a point which arose in our second visit to Brussels. One Commission official explained that simplified legislation (referred to as "less Brussels, more Member States") did not always lead to better implementation: it often allowed for a greater degree of interpretation by the Member States, and that was typically where the problems arose (Q 469).

36. Commissioner Charlie McCreevy confirmed this view: "Directives are an overarching type of a framework. They allow Member States a fair degree of flexibility. Most Member States add rather than subtract and most Member States gold-plate rather than take away". The result is a bit of a "mish-mash". Regulations on the other hand, which pass directly into European law, have the exact same effect in 27 Member States and safeguard against interpretation by Member States as well as gold-plating. However, Member States were very reluctant to agree to prescriptive regulations at EU level (Q 474).

37. The patchy implementation of Single Market rules is compounded by the uneven provision made by Member States for National Regulatory Authorities (NRAs). The Committee was surprised to discover that the powers and remit of NRAs vary considerably between Member States since "there is no European model of how the National Regulatory Authorities ... should actually be set up" (Dr Mark Thatcher Q 29). Crucially, there is also no legislation regarding the need for independence from government, which was a recurring source of concern in the evidence received, across all three sectors (see paragraphs 90 and 110). Many witnesses called for closer cooperation between national regulators, in order to ensure a more even interpretation and application of the rules across the Member States; this was considered an essential pre-requisite to increasing cross-border activity, especially among SMEs (see paragraphs 44–46).

---

7 Scoreboard 16, Internal Market, July 2007

8 *Ibid.*

38. Given the difficulties inherent in agreeing and implementing legislation, it was not surprising that Commissioner McCreevy described himself as very reluctant to go down the legislative route in future. Quite apart from issues concerning interpretation and implementation, the process is very lengthy, inevitably so given the number of Member States involved. Mr McCreevy advocated "effective [non-legislative] action" (Q 474).

39. The Committee was given the impression from a number of witnesses that the construction of the Single Market had developed sufficiently so that a lot of new legislation was no longer required. Mr Bryan Cassidy, member of the Single Market Observatory (of the European Economic and Social Committee) commented that "the big battles were fought and won some considerable time ago … Compared with the heady days of 1991 we are now down to much more workaday and detailed things" (Q 415). Mr Jean-Claude Thebault, Deputy-Head of the Cabinet of the President of the Commission, confirmed this view, saying that "we are not in a period where we have to issue many directives or regulations" (Q 398).

40. The Committee heard from Commission officials that they are keen to "build up a more preventative and proactive approach upstream" (Q 204), focusing on assisting Member States early on in the transposition process, rather than waiting until such a time when infringement proceedings need to be commenced. Concrete steps are already being taken in this direction with the publication of a handbook to assist Member States with the implementation of the Services Directive[9].

Problem-solving in the Single Market

41. SOLVIT, a dispute resolution mechanism, is another example of an initiative launched under this objective. SOLVIT was set up in 2002 as a problem solving network to handle complaints arising from the misapplication of EU rules by public authorities. The Committee heard evidence from Commission officials charged with the coordination of the SOLVIT network and was very impressed by the work that such centres undertake. There are 30 national SOLVIT centres, based in the Member States and also in members of the European Free Trade Area (Iceland, Lichtenstein, Norway). Levels of staffing and general resources are at the discretion of Member States and as a result these vary widely. SOLVIT assesses the staffing levels in offices as either "adequate" or "low". In its 2006 report it rated the UK as "adequate".

42. The SOLVIT network exists without any formal legal basis—it was set up following a Council recommendation, and its activities are dependent on the cooperation of Member States and relevant authorities (Q 423). To date this approach appears to be very successful, with over 80% of cases being solved.

43. Although SOLVIT exists to resolve disputes, a large amount of submitted complaints are actually requests for information about cross-border matters without any actual dispute. These complaints, making up around 80% of submissions, are most often about "the impossibility of finding decent information about what the rules are". Ms Marian Grubben, the SOLVIT team leader, described this information gap as "maybe the single most important problem for SMEs" (Q 425).

---

9 The Handbook can be found at: http://ec.europa.eu/internal_market/services/services-dir/index_en.htm

SMEs and the Single Market

44. The Committee sought evidence on the barriers likely to be encountered by SMEs in trying to take advantage of the Single Market. The Committee took evidence from the Federation of Small Businesses (FSB) that only 2% of UK SMEs were conducting business in other EU markets (Q 83), which suggested that barriers were very high indeed. The FSB referred to the Single Market as a "remarkable success story" but that "the small business community has yet to share in its benefits" (Q 66). Ms Karen Clements, from the British Chambers of Commerce (BCC), referred to a growing "disenchantment" with the European Union and the Single Market amongst the members of the BCC because "businesses are not reaping the full benefits of the Single Market" (Q 66).

45. The role of Member States and their responsibility for implementation and enforcement was cited as one of the main barriers: "the persistent national abuse of Single Market principles, whether it is flouting the principle of mutual recognition or failing to implement and enforce laws on time and evenly" (Q 66). A further barrier was the lack of a single source of reliable information about trading across Member States (Q 68), and this had led to a lack of confidence about entering other EU markets (Q 70). This point was supported by evidence from Ms Grubben, the SOLVIT team leader, who felt there was "an enormous need for more user-friendly targeted information for businesses just about practical things—where do I go to achieve this, what sort of forms do I need to fill in" (Q 425).

46. Both the FSB and the BCC referred to the importance of completing the internal market in services: in its written evidence the FSB stated that 99.8% of EU businesses are SMEs, of which 89% operate in the service sector (p 39). It was hoped that the Services Directive would enhance levels of engagement with the Single Market among SMEs (Q 101). Both the BCC and the FSB expressed disappointment with the final form of the Services Directive, which had been significantly weakened by the time of agreement. Mr Clive Davenport, representing the FSB, argued that the impact for SMEs was effectively to "keep [them] out of the Single Market, or at least make entry complicated and expensive for them" (Q 111).

Economic Nationalism and the Country of Origin Principle

47. The Committee was concerned from the outset of this inquiry by the apparent incidence of economic nationalism in Europe, by some Member States resisting the adoption of liberalisation measures, in markets such as energy and telecoms, in an effort to protect national industries (the so-called "national champions"). Such action appeared to us contrary to the principles of the Single Market; many of our witnesses agreed.

48. The CBI wrote that "the recent trend of protectionism in the EU, whether in the name of protecting national champions or economic nationalism, is contrary to the four principles of the European Union" (p 216). Evidence submitted by Malcolm Harbour MEP, John Purvis MEP and Baroness Wilcox warned that economic nationalism posed a threat to EU competitiveness. The Government argued that such measures, although designed to protect domestic industries and avoid job losses, were "directly threatening to open and competitive markets, and will not protect jobs and growth in the long term" (p 145).

49. The Committee heard evidence from Mr Peter Sutherland (former EU Commissioner for Competition, and Chairman of BP and Goldman Sachs International) who argued that while economic nationalism was not new, the articulation of it had recently changed in an attempt to render it more acceptable: "the arguments about national champions have been couched in phrases which at least recognises the European nature of the champion rather than the national nature of the champion" (Q 318).

50. Evidence received from the FSB referred to the "serious threat posed" to the Single Market by the protectionist tendencies of some stakeholders and Member States and highlighted in particular the "sustained attempt to undermine the country of origin principle" (FSB p 40). The "country of origin principle" has been the legislative building block for the facilitation of free movement of goods or services across borders. This principle has underpinned efforts to increase competitiveness within the EU by making it possible for businesses to trade in other Member States on the basis of "home country" regulations. The Government's evidence referred to it as an "important tool" in delivering the freedom of movement for goods and services, and in "providing legal certainty" for businesses which would otherwise have to comply with different rules and regulations when operating across borders (p 144). Dr Thatcher added that without the country of origin principle we run the risk of back-sliding toward a state of non-tariff barriers and national protectionism (Q 36)[10].

51. This was a view shared by many witnesses, who also expressed their disappointment at the outcome of negotiations on the Services Directive. Witnesses argued that the Directive had led to a significant dilution of the country of origin principle (BCC, FSB, CBI). In the Services Directive the principle is only applicable to companies operating in a host country on a temporary basis. Once they become established in another Member State they must comply with that country's regulations. However, the nature of a temporary basis was not clearly defined. The FSB argued that as a result of the "nebulous" text of the Services Directive the Single Market in services would have to be achieved through recourse to the European Court of Justice (p 40). The CBI expressed concern that the Directive would act as a deterrent to businesses, especially SMEs wishing to operate in other EU Member States (p 216).

52. The Committee has previously expressed its support for the country of origin principle in its reports on the Services Directive and the Audio-Visual Media Directive[11]. It has been concerned by the potential for the dilution of the country of origin principle to adversely affect businesses, both SMEs and larger companies.

Consumers and the Single Market

53. Despite the broader benefits to citizens in terms of free movement and the right to study, work or retire abroad, which were mentioned by the

---

[10] The Committee took the view in its report The Services Directive Revisited that "many of the concerns expressed about a 'race to the bottom' in terms of employment conditions would be met by the overriding application of the Posting of Workers Directive (Directive 96/71/EC) to employees posted to work in another Member State. The effect of this would be that such employees would be covered by the laws and regulations relating to employment in the host country" (paragraph 16).

[11] European Union Committee, 38th report (2005–06): *The Services Directive Revisited* (HL 215); European Union Committee, 3rd report (2006–07): *Television without Frontiers* (HL 27).

Commission (see paragraph 27 above), as consumers some citizens do not perceive the Single Market as a reality (Q 216). There are two aspects to this—the failure of cross-border purchasing to develop beyond very marginal activity; and the failure of key markets, such as energy, to be sufficiently liberalised at national level for consumers to enjoy the benefit of increased competition (Q 218).

54. We received evidence from BEUC, the European Consumers Organisation, and the National Consumer Council (NCC) which suggested that the key to improving consumer confidence in cross-border shopping was to provide consumers with the same level of consumer protection, including proper means of redress, as when shopping at home (Q 218). On the other hand, other factors may be at work—consumer resistance is not unfounded, but reflects practical and cultural factors which make cross-border shopping less attractive. Mr Dominique Forest concurred that what really mattered were the concrete benefits to consumers that could arise from "providers from other Member States settling in your country and making the home market more competitive" (Q 221). This required the proper implementation of liberalisation measures across the Member States (Q 223).

Economic and Monetary Union[12]

55. The Committee sought evidence of the impact of Economic and Monetary Union (EMU) and the adoption of the euro in 13 of the Member States on the functioning of the Single Market. The Commission pointed to the benefits of increased transparency and reduction in the cost of cross-border activities as a result of the single currency. The Government conceded that the single currency could play a role in strengthening transparency, and that the elimination of exchange rate risk and transaction costs under EMU facilitated the provision of cross-border financial services (p 145). The benefit of transparency was supported by BEUC, the European consumers' organisation, but it was also pointed out that transparency needs to be accompanied by very concrete measures to make it beneficial to consumers; the euro in itself cannot deal with the lack of competition, or the difficulties in cross-border shopping, or with uncertainties about the rights and means of redress for consumers (Q 219).

56. Another impact suggested by witnesses was an increase in foreign direct investment. The Centre for European Policy Studies (CEPS) argued that the introduction of the single currency has been one of the major factors in increasing the attractiveness of the European financial market (p 207). Mr Sutherland argued that inward investment to the UK would have been higher if the UK was part of the eurozone (Q 319). Lord Williamson of Horton made the point that currency variations in the Single Market can present difficulties (Q 7), but he conceded that there did not appear to be a problem for businesses crossing over from the eurozone to the sterling zone (Q 13).

57. Dr Thatcher told us that a single currency may help the functioning of the Single Market, but it is not a necessary or sufficient condition for its success (Q 46). He argued that the lack of common standards was a more important barrier than the lack of a common currency.

---

[12] EMU is considered in greater detail in our report forthcoming report on the issue.

CHAPTER 4: GENERAL CONCLUSIONS

58. This chapter contains general conclusions arising from our consideration of the issues affecting the Single Market as a whole, and supported by the findings in each of the individual sectors examined. Specific recommendations are made for each of the sectors in the following chapters, but are not repeated here.

59. We believe that the Single Market has great potential to deliver benefits to consumers and businesses, and yet, despite its impressive record, its future appears at risk. We are concerned that the momentum behind the Single Market has been weakened. **We therefore call on the Government and the Commission to instil a sense of urgency into the review of the Single Market. Despite substantial gains to date, without renewed political commitment to making the Single Market a reality, there is a risk of sliding backwards.**

60. Less legislation: there is little appetite for new legislation to be introduced—many witnesses concurred on this point, including the Commission. There was also support for the increased use of non-legislative tools such as self-regulation to help overcome the difficulties of legislating for an expanded EU. **The Committee strongly supports the Commission's commitment, made in the Single Market Review, to keep legislation simple, to roll back EU intervention where it is no longer appropriate, and to seek non-legislative solutions where possible.**

61. The failure of Member States to implement Single Market legislation damages businesses and consumers: the evidence overwhelmingly argued that existing rules are not being effectively implemented across the 27 Member States. The responsibility for implementing and enforcing the Single Market lies with Member States, starting with the timely and proper transposition of directives. The impetus, the political will and the drive to follow up commitments with proper implementation must come from the Member States; the failure to do so puts the whole Single Market at risk. **The Commission's Review rightly emphasises the importance of working in partnership with Member States and local authorities, but this Committee would place greater onus on the Member States to meet their commitments in order to achieve a fully-functioning Single Market.**

62. Effective policy-making underlies good implementation: policies that are based on detailed sector-specific understanding, derived from consultation with industry, civil society and Member State governments, are more likely to be relevant and therefore easier to implement. **We therefore welcome the Commission's proposals in its Review of the Single Market for better product and sector monitoring, consultation with a wider range of stakeholders and improved impact assessments.**

63. Commission as facilitator: in a European Union of 27 Member States the Commission has to play the role of facilitator and enabler. **More effort and resources should be devoted to providing practical assistance to Member States in the process of transposing legislation in order to avoid problems of interpretation, delayed implementation or failure to enforce later on.**

64. However, our evidence also suggested that the Commission should make better use of its powers, including its competition powers, in cases where cooperation is not forthcoming. **The focus on assisting Member States early on in the process of transposition must not come at the expense of effective enforcement when necessary.**

65. **We welcome therefore the Commission's proposals for a more proactive approach to prevent problems in the implementation of EU law, promoting best practice through a Member State working group and supporting the exchange of information and staff between national administrations, as well as using competition powers, such as sector inquiries.**

66. **National Regulatory Authorities must be independent of government, especially where governments have financial interests in the major market operator or national incumbent.** This is essential to generate consumer and market confidence, and is the best way to ensure a fair application of the rules. The powers of regulators should also be reviewed in light of the broad diversity of scope and remits. These are areas where new EU legislation may be appropriate.

67. **There is no need for a 'super-regulator' at EU-level in any of the sectors we considered in this inquiry.** National market differences make this undesirable. However, there is a need for greater and better coordination between national regulatory authorities, especially in matters regarding the cross-border provision of services. This is essential if market access is to become a reality—especially for consumers and SMEs.

68. **The Committee is pleased to see that the Commission's recent proposals suggest more cooperation between National Regulatory Authorities; the need for operational independence of regulators; and strengthened powers for regulators to ensure that consumers and businesses can reap the benefits of the Single Market.**

69. **More should be done to help SMEs participate actively in the Single Market**. Very few SMEs are engaged in cross-border activity and this is largely due to the regulatory barriers which remain in place, and the lack of reliable information to assist businesses. The Commission has made the objective of engaging small business in the Single Market the centre-piece of its Review and this is to be welcomed and supported.

70. Winning hearts and minds: evidence indicated that values and social benefits are as important to reconnect Europe with its citizens as are economic advantages. **Consumers and citizens need to be more fully persuaded of the benefits of the Single Market**. The Commission must ensure that clear and accessible information is available about these social benefits as well as the economic benefits. We welcome the right of all European citizens to petition the Commission directly and feel that this should be extended to include matters of consumer redress. The Commission's Review rightly includes many proposals designed to make the Single Market more accessible to the consumer, as well as to make its benefits better known to the consumer.

71. Free and undistorted competition to continue: The Minister for Europe assured the Committee that the removal of the words free and undistorted competition from the text of the Reform Treaty had not led, and would not

lead, to a change in policy[13]. This was supported by evidence heard from Commission officials. However, we continue to be concerned by evidence of support for "national champions" in some Member States. We agree with the Government that such practices are contrary to the principles of the Single Market and will not benefit consumers or businesses. **We call for a renewed commitment to the importance of competition and the need to complete the Single Market for the benefit of consumers and businesses alike.**

13 European Union Committee, 28th Report (2006–07): *Evidence from the Minister for Europe on the June European Council and the 2007 Inter-Governmental Conference* (HL 142)

CHAPTER 5: ENERGY

Introduction

72. This chapter of the report considers the operation and progress of the Single Market within the energy sector. This part of the inquiry received the most submissions of evidence, and it was also the sector which proved the most controversial. During the course of our inquiry the Commission published its 3rd legislative package on the energy and gas markets—much of the evidence received was in anticipation of those proposals.

Benefits of a Single Market in Energy

73. Competition within Europe's energy markets is central to the three interlinked policy objectives of a competitive and efficient energy sector, security of supply, and sustainability of energy sources.

Competition and Efficiency

74. In our view, competitive and efficient markets are central to ensuring that citizens pay a fair price for their energy needs. High and volatile energy prices cause disproportionate hardship to vulnerable customers and reduce the competitiveness of some businesses. The FSB reported that SMEs are under "particular strain in a volatile energy market and this is coupled with unclear pricing policies and poor standards of service" (p 41). A recent npower survey[14], referred to in the FSB's evidence, reflected this view.

75. Respondents also provided evidence that imperfect competition leads to under-investment, hindering the effective operation of the market and reinforcing the lack of competition. Centrica pointed to examples of longstanding network congestion between Member States perpetuated by under-investment (Q 181). Under investment in network connection has also inhibited new entrants to the market. Furthermore, network reliability is also affected (National Grid claim that UK transmission network reliability is significantly greater than that of Continental Europe[15]).

Security of Supply

76. There are well documented examples of gas flows between Member States temporarily not moving in the direction expected given the relative market prices in those states. A number of witnesses, including Centrica and National Grid, consequently highlighted the importance of further energy market liberalisation in ensuring security of supply against this kind of apparently anti-competitive behaviour.

77. Such essentially short term occurrences are not however necessarily indicative of uncompetitive behaviour. Shell provided evidence that energy markets, particularly gas markets, are largely long term in nature, whereas the regulatory focus tends to analyse short term signals and behaviours. They argue instead that long term gas supply contracts are central to Europe's security of supply (p 236).

---

14 npower is part of the RWE Group, a multi-utility energy company.

15 National Grid's response to the Communication from the Commissions: "An Energy Policy for Europe" COM(07)1. This is available from the Parliamentary Archives.

Sustainability of Energy Sources and Climate Change

78. Witnesses supported the need for a market-based approach to meeting the Commission's climate change objectives, through the EU Emission Trading Scheme (EU ETS), for example. For such mechanisms to work effectively energy markets need to be undistorted. The Association for Electricity Producers commented that "The completion of the Single Market is therefore necessary so that a level playing field can be achieved throughout Member States and carbon price drivers can act uniformly across Europe" (p 194).

79. The European Regulators Group for Electricity and Gas (ERGEG) highlighted the role of regulation in creating a stable and predictable context for private sector investment in new, green technologies. To achieve this investment, the market needs to provide longer term signals on carbon prices that can be factored into investment appraisal and analysis (Q 238). Within Europe, these signals are predicated on the length and terms of EU commitment to mechanisms like the EU ETS.

Restrictions to Effective Competition

80. It is widely felt that existing EU legislation[16], and its degree of transposition into national law by Member States, has not yet achieved the objectives of market opening and citizens have yet to benefit fully from a single energy market. We note the European Commission's recent work to investigate the root causes of restrictions to effective competition and their draft proposals to address them. The Commission's Energy Sector Inquiry was published on 10 January 2007[17] and was followed on 19 September by proposals for a 3rd package of legislation to address the shortcomings in market functioning.

81. A number of our witnesses supported the findings of the European Commission's Energy Sector Inquiry. In particular, the Office of Gas and Electricity Markets (Ofgem) and Centrica drew attention to a range of significant problems, highlighted in the Inquiry, that were preventing effective competition emerging. These included: market concentration; collusion between incumbents to share markets; vertical integration; lack of access to infrastructure; lack of or delayed investment; and a lack of market transparency that is preventing new entrants from assessing the scope for profitable entry (Centrica p 72).

82. Ofgem also highlighted the limited scope of existing EU rules to address many cross-border issues, as well as their uneven and insufficient implementation by Member States. It argued that a 'regulatory gap' has been created which acts as a serious impediment to investment and cross-border trade (p 22).

Proposed Solutions to Restrictions on Competition

83. From the evidence received, four main themes emerge as central to the debate over how to facilitate effective competition in EU energy markets: legislation; unbundling; regulation; and market transparency.

---

16 For example, the Second Electricity and Gas Directives, respectively 2003/54/EC and 2003/55/EC

17 DG Competition Report on Energy Sector Inquiry 10 January 2007 (SEC(2006) 1724)

Legislation

84. The Commission has proposed a 3rd package of energy legislation. A number of witnesses, including Ofgem, the former DTI and HM Treasury, support the need for further legislation, particularly to mandate ownership unbundling, as discussed in more detail below (paragraphs 86–89). However, the view was not shared by all. Some respondents cautioned against the enactment of new laws before reviewing, and ensuring compliance with, existing legislation (CBI p 215, Shell p 234).

85. Market investigations and sanctions against anti-competitive and protectionist behaviour in the private sector were supported by a number of witnesses, as were infringement actions by the Commission against Member States that failed to enact and enforce EU legislation (AEP p 193, Centrica p 73, DTI p 144)[18]. CBI noted, in respect of internal market legislation, that the "patchwork implementation [by Member States] has resulted in a number of national barriers remaining in place, restricting companies from truly benefiting from the advantages of a fully functioning internal market" (p 215). In their view, this situation is particularly evident in the area of energy policy where the market remains highly fragmented.

Unbundling

86. Unbundling network assets from supply interests is the most significant and controversial of the proposed solutions to restrictions on effective competition. The argument is that whilst the ownership of energy transmission networks is controlled within the same vertically integrated group as a supply business, an inherent conflict of interest arises. This is between network investment or operational decisions which might benefit diversity of supply within the market and the competitive advantage enjoyed by the related supply business if that diversity is suppressed. The conflict also extends to preferential network and information access.

87. In practice, two separation models emerge as possible solutions to such a conflict; full ownership unbundling or an independent system operator model. Full ownership unbundling is where a group cannot have a controlling interest in both network and supply businesses in the same market. The independent system operator (ISO) model is where a group can have majority ownership in both, but all strategic, managerial and operational decisions in respect of the transmission network are licensed to an independent third party. The ISO model requires comprehensive regulatory oversight to be effective.

88. With the exception of Gaz de France (Q 178), all respondents were in favour of a greater separation of transmission and supply interests. The majority favoured full ownership unbundling, including National Grid who have direct experience of both models in the UK. National Grid argue that the ownership unbundling method has delivered significant benefits in the UK in terms of levels of investment, removing network congestion, non-discriminatory third party access, reliability and transparency. National Grid cautioned against promotion of the ISO model for which they point out there is limited precedent within gas markets[19].

---

18 We note the infringement action against 20 Member States by the Commission in April 2006 and subsequent issue of 26 "reasoned opinions" in December 2006 to 16 Member States in respect of their failure to implement the Second electricity and gas directives in full.

19 *Op. Cit.*

89. Gaz de France provided oral evidence that continued integration of transmission and supply interests achieves a larger critical mass within the organisation, which is advantageous when negotiating supply contracts with dominant third country suppliers, such as those from Russia. In their view, integration and further market consolidation were central to the security of Europe's energy supply (Q 178). We also heard evidence from POWEO, a small operator in the French energy market, offering integrated electricity and gas services predominantly to business clients. Mr Frédéric Granotier, co-founder of POWEO, maintained that "complete separation of the network from incumbents ... would of course help competition because we always fear that there exist cross-subsidies between activities" (Q 385). He argued that full unbundling offered the best scenario, as there would be more transparency and no conflict of interest (Q 390). However, he conceded that for political or historical reasons this situation was unlikely to be achieved in France, and that the ISO model, if properly policed, could also remove the risk of conflict of interest or cross-subsidies (Q 390).

Regulation

90. A number of respondents referred to the divergence amongst Member States in the authority and powers of regulators, and their degree of separation from both industry and government. It is noted that in Member States with strong, independent regulation, the degree of liberalisation and level of competition is further advanced.

91. An overwhelming number of respondents called for greater co-operation of national energy regulators but there was no support for a European regulator. The Commission itself commented that "we do not need to have a European regulator that will replace national regulators; on the contrary, we still need strong national regulators and the regulatory function at EU level should be there to strengthen the national regulators, not to replace the national regulators" (Q 213). Instead, it has proposed the establishment of an agency for the cooperation of national energy regulators to coordinate the frameworks within which national regulators and network operators cooperate. The agency's powers would be limited to resolving cross-border investment issues, combined with an advisory role to refer matters to the Commission.

Market Transparency

92. Free access to market information for all current and would-be participants is essential to an efficient market. Market transparency is currently limited to network capacity, informing participants if capacity is available, and if all available capacity is being offered. Vertically integrated utilities have greater access to information on, for example, the level of gas stocks, forecast demand and supply, and trading positions, giving them a potential competitive advantage over new entrants or less integrated participants. This assessment is supported by the FSB who submitted evidence that the "greatest barrier small businesses face entering the internal market is access to reliable information" (p 39).

93. This is not to say that company specific or commercially sensitive information should be publicised, a concern raised by Shell who support transparency where it serves a purpose (p 234). However, market

information available solely within large, vertically integrated utilities, purely by virtue of that integration, goes against the principle of competition.

94. A number of respondents supported greater record-keeping by market participants regarding operational decisions and trades, and provision of information to regulators to enable market monitoring at a European level. CBI called for greater action by national administrators, the European Commission, national courts, and the European Court of Justice to improve monitoring of the functioning of Internal Market rules (p 216).

Conclusions for the Energy Sector

95. Good progress has been made in the liberalisation of EU energy markets, but that progress is not uniform across the Member States, and as a consequence, the benefits to consumers are restricted. **The package of legislation proposed by the Commission is welcomed by the Committee as it is necessary to address, in particular, the practice of some network operators to discriminate against third parties in favour of their own related supply interests.**

96. **Having considered the evidence, we are of the opinion that full ownership unbundling more satisfactorily removes the incentives for discriminatory and uncompetitive behaviour by the network operator**. To deliver just some of the benefits of ownership unbundling, the ISO model requires a level of regulation and monitoring which simply is not in place in a number of Member States.

97. There needs to be a stronger, more independent and more co-ordinated EU approach to regulation. This, combined with greater access to market information and a tough line against uncompetitive behaviour, will propel Europe further towards the key policy objectives of competition and efficiency, security of supply and sustainability. **Therefore, we support the creation of an agency for the cooperation of NRAs but would reject calls for a European regulatory authority.**

98. The Committee notes the concern raised by Gaz de France that unbundling the market may lead to a weakening of the negotiating position of the EU, as a single entity, in relation to large third country suppliers. **We accept that security of supply is important but we are not convinced that the creation of a more comprehensive Single Market in energy would necessarily weaken international supply.**

CHAPTER 6: TELECOMMUNICATIONS

Introduction

99. This chapter considers the state of the EU telecommunications sector. Less evidence was received in respect of this sector than the others, which is understandable given the progress already made towards a Single Market in telecommunications. During the course of our inquiry proposals from the Commission for reform of the sector were published on 13 November 2007[20]. These proposals had been anticipated in the evidence received and, to a large extent, in the findings presented below.

Telecommunication Markets

100. The telecommunications sector falls into three distinct markets: telecommunications equipment, service, and network infrastructure. The pace of liberalisation has differed between the different markets, with the equipment market having become a global marketplace in which EU-based companies are prominent. For telecommunication services, newly emerging services, such as the provision of Internet access, have been highly competitive from the start, while traditional voice telephony services have experienced fewer competitive pressures. The degree of competition in the provision of network infrastructure varies significantly between the Member States, due both to differing levels of economic development, particularly in the new Accession States, and to different Member State priorities.

EU Regulation and Market Liberalisation

101. The telecommunications industry has undergone a fundamental change in structure, from that of monopoly to one of competition. Much of EU law and regulation in the sector has been concerned with this process of change: regulating to encourage competition. In July 2003 the New Regulatory Framework (widely referred to as the NRF) came into force. The NRF is designed to embrace all forms of communication or transmission technology, whether used to carry voice calls, Internet traffic or television programmes; while the concept of telecommunications has been replaced by the concepts of 'electronic communications networks' and 'electronic communications services'. The reform proposals published during our inquiry would result in a wide range of amendments to the NRF designed to improve its operation; complete the development of a single European market; and enhance the rights and protections for consumers and users[21]. However, the reforms do not constitute a fundamental realignment of the current regime.

102. While liberalisation initiatives have aimed at opening up national markets to competition, harmonisation measures are required to address competition across markets in the EU. Harmonisation between Member State markets has inevitably involved greater complexity and detailed regulatory intervention than that required for the liberalisation of national markets.

---

20 Available at http://ec.europa.eu/information_society/policy/ecomm/tomorrow/index_en.htm

21 Communication from the Commission, 'Report on the outcome of the Review of the EU regulatory framework for electronic communications networks and services in accordance with Directive 2002/21/EC and Summary of the 2007 Reform Proposals', COM(2007)696.

Barriers to a Single Market

103. There continue to be a number of barriers to the achievement of a Single Market in telecommunications. First, the national nature of the consumer markets means that trans-national operators cannot usually offer single products across a number of Member States. Second, the legacy position of national incumbents within national markets also seems to be a barrier to the achievement of a Single Market for telecommunications. For example, despite over 20 years of competition in the UK market, BT continues to dominate certain traditional market segments, such as residential fixed voice telephony. In its reform proposals, the Commission notes that incumbents continue to remain dominant in the area of fixed telephony (with an average market share of 65.8%), as well as in the broadband internet access market (generally over 55%)[22]. Incumbent operators have successfully leveraged their position in their domestic markets to enter and compete with incumbent operators in other national markets. So, for example, France Telecom (through Orange), Deutsche Telecom (through T-Mobile) and Telefonica of Spain (through O2) all have a significant presence in the UK market. While such incumbent operators do compete, there is also potential them to favour the status quo, rather than campaigning for radical regulatory intervention in the European market that would be viewed as undesirable in the domestic marketplace.

104. Furthermore, Member States continue to exercise considerable discretion over a number of areas that impact directly or indirectly on the development of national markets, which then impinge on the Single Market project. Different approaches to the allocation of 3G spectrum, for example, resulted in a wide variance of national practice which in turn has resulted in differences in the roll-out and market for 3G services between Member States.

105. As with every area of the Single Market, the nature of the law reform process within the Community means that Member States retain considerable flexibility in the transposition of EU measures. An inevitable consequence of this is continued existence of divergent approaches in the application of certain Community measures. One key element of the Commission's reform proposals is to improve co-ordination between Member State national regulatory authorities, partly through the establishment of an independent European Electronic Communications Market Authority (see below, paragraph 113).

State of Markets

106. The general impression given by witnesses is that the EU has achieved much in terms of a Single Market in telecommunications. Progress has been particularly spectacular in the market for telecommunications equipment. Where liberalisation of markets has already been progressed some witnesses were certain that it has provided "significant opportunities for cross border investment" (BT p 202).

107. Historically both regulators and operators have viewed telecommunications markets as, "to a large extent, national markets" (T-Mobile p 238) with Member States responsible for "co-ordination between themselves and on

---

22 *Ibid.*

cross-border interference" (Ofcom p 18). Ofcom, however, notes that the increasing use of IP technologies[23] means that services could "in theory, be offered from anywhere in the EU to anywhere else, without there being any need for the service provider to have a physical presence in the country where the service is being used. This offers the possibility of a genuinely new, pan-European telecoms service market developing" (p 20).

108. British Telecom expressed concern that as the market changes the country of origin principle would continue to be important. Were it to be weakened British Telecom envisaged a situation where "an online service provider has to be aware of 27 different sets of national rules and thus may shy away from providing pan-EU services" (p 202).

Regulatory Framework

109. Calls for reform centre primarily on issues relating to "inadequate enforcement and widely diverging application of the rules" (CBI p 217), rather than the substantive provisions themselves, which generally receive widespread approval.

110. A number of witnesses expressed concern that NRAs in certain Member States, particularly in the new Accession states, were not sufficiently resourced or independent from government to carry out their functions satisfactorily (BT p 201, Ofcom p 22). NRAs in the telecommunications sector have played a key role in assisting the process of liberalisation and harmonisation within the EU. However, independence has proved difficult in a number of Member States, particularly in terms of political influence. British Telecom saw "a strong correlation between continued state ownership of former monopoly operators and inadequate implementation and enforcement of EU telecoms regulation" (p 202).

111. British Telecom in their evidence also suggested that the development of pan-European services for business has been constrained by the failure of national incumbents to provide suitable "local access" products (p 202). They argued that this is due to the debate on EU telecoms regulation focussing on "the needs of residential telecoms users rather than major business customers" (p 202).

Modernisation

112. As noted above, the main concerns raised by respondents relate to the implementation of the existing rules, rather than the rules themselves. The Commission has recently reviewed the current regime and proposed certain substantive and procedural revisions. Overall, the Commission's reform proposals have been welcomed by respondents. Ofcom argued that access to spectrum was an increasingly important and valuable commodity and stated that it was necessary to find ways of accurately valuing and efficiently allocating spectrum (p 18). Some witnesses argued that this was best achieved through reconciling the needs for spectrum harmonisation, to avoid interference between services, with a flexible approach to usage. Proposals to both harmonise and liberalise spectrum management[24], for example, met with support (CEPS pp 210–211, Harbour, Purvis, Wilcox p 223).

---

23 "IP" stands for Internet Protocol. In telecoms IP technologies are those that operate over the internet, such as Skype.

24 Reaping the full benefits of the digital dividend in Europe: A common approach to the use of the spectrum released by the digital switchover COM (2007) 700 final.

113. The one point on which witnesses disagreed with the Commission concerns centralised EU regulation mechanisms. Viviane Reding, the Commissioner for the Information Society, has proposed the establishment of the 'European Electronic Communications Market Authority'[25], to address issues with a pan-European dimension rather than the current system of co-operation between NRAs. Nearly all respondents expressed concern or hostility towards this proposal, considering that the European Regulators Group (ERG), comprising representatives of the 27 Member State NRAs, is capable of operating in an appropriate manner (BT p 203, CBI p 218, Ofcom pp 21–22, T-Mobile p 237). Despite the current inconsistency between Member States, witnesses like Ofcom (p 21) and the CBI argued that NRAs "are closest to the market and ultimately should be best placed to make regulatory decisions", whereas a "Euro-regulator" would simply add an unnecessary "additional layer of policy or decision-making on top of the existing institutional arrangements" (CBI p 218). Commission officials told us that the proposal was aimed at "improving the better functioning of national regulators and improving their cooperation among themselves" (Q 406). But it was not clear why a new level of authority, with the power to make recommendations to the Commission to veto remedies proposed by an NRA, was necessary to achieve this aim.

Conclusions for the Telecommunications Sector

114. The policy to liberalise and harmonise the telecommunications markets for the provision of networks, services and equipment has been substantially successful, particularly in the services and equipment markets. Such developments have contributed to the very considerable rate of technical and market innovation experienced in the sector over recent years, which has resulted in extensive economic and social benefits accruing to EU citizens.

115. In general, the current regulatory framework for the provision of electronic communications networks and services has met its objectives and does not require any radical revision. **The main concern continues to be failures by Member States in the implementation and enforcement of certain elements of their regulatory obligations**. The Commission has recognised this in its reform proposals, with new measures designed to improve its oversight of the decisions of Member State NRAs, to ensure greater consistency in approach between Member States. We therefore welcome its reform proposals in this respect.

116. **The Commission should consider what steps can be taken to reduce further the market power of the national incumbents**. Functional separation, where an operator places the provision of certain wholesale access products in an independently operated business unit supplying all market players on equal terms and conditions, including the operator's own retail business, provides a potential model that should be considered by NRAs for other incumbent operators. This approach was voluntarily implemented by BT through Openreach. The Committee supports the Commission's proposal to enable NRAs to impose this as a remedy[26].

117. **The Committee was not persuaded that the Commission's proposal to establish an EU regulator for the telecommunications sector is**

---

25 COM(2007)699 rev 2, 13 November 2007.

26 COM(2007)697 rev 1.

necessary. The ERG is a co-ordinating agency similar to what has been proposed for the energy sector. Despite the claims made by the Commission, the Committee believe that such a measure is likely to increase regulatory complexity and uncertainty for market participants and bring insufficient benefits for the costs involved.

118. Ensuring that spectrum management is flexible enough to meet the challenges of technological advances was raised to some witnesses. **We therefore welcome the Commission's initiative on spectrum, including the facilitation of secondary trading; greater access to licence-free spectrum, and further co-ordination on the conditions applicable to spectrum authorisations**.

CHAPTER 7: FINANCIAL SERVICES

Introduction

119. This section addresses the issues relating to the Single Market in financial services, an area in which the Committee feels that the lack of progress has been disappointing. Our inquiry coincided with the Commission's consultation on retail financial services, which resulted in proposals for measures on retail financial services in the Commission's review of the Single Market[27], and inevitably this aspect featured prominently in the submissions received, and therefore, in our findings.

Overview of Regulatory Developments

120. During most of the 1990s, efforts in the financial services sector were largely focused on achieving a smooth transition to the single European currency, with the broader issue of the functioning of the EU financial markets having a lesser priority. In May 1999, the Commission published a Communication containing a Financial Services Action Plan (FSAP)[28], which the Lisbon European Council endorsed in March 2000.

121. The FSAP is a set of 42 legislative measures intended to fill gaps and remove barriers to create a legal and regulatory environment supporting the integration of EU financial markets. It has three aims:

- the creation of a single EU wholesale market for financial services and products;
- the creation of an open and secure financial retail market; and
- implementation of state of the art prudential rules and supervision.

122. The FSAP was largely completed by its 2004 deadline, with 39 of the 42 measures adopted.[29] The next stage of FSAP involves the implementation of the measures into national law, as some of the measures were only due to be implemented by late 2007. Witnesses agree that "it is too early to assess the full costs of the programme ... let alone the benefits to the economies of Europe attributable to the FSAP" (FSA p 16).

123. Since the FSAP focused mainly on the wholesale market, the Commission identified the completion of the retail financial services market as one of its key priorities. In May 2007 it published a Green Paper on Retail Financial Services, which set out its objectives of furthering integration in EU retail financial services markets by:

- ensuring that properly regulated open markets and strong competition deliver products that meet consumers' needs, offering choice, value and quality;
- enhancing consumer confidence by ensuring that consumers are properly protected where appropriate, and that providers are financially sound and trustworthy; and

---

27 'Initiatives in the area of retail financial services', Accompanying document to the Communication from the Commission to the European Parliament, the Council, the European Economic and Social Committee and the Committee of the Regions, SEC(2007) 1520.

28 Financial Services: Implementing the framework for financial markets: Action Plan, Communication from the Commission.

29 FSAP Evaluation: Part I: Process and implementation, Commission (p 3).

- empowering consumers to make the right decisions for their financial circumstances through improved financial literacy; clear, appropriate and timely information; high-quality advice; and a level playing field between products perceived as having similar characteristics.[30]

124. On 20 November 2007, as part of the Single Market review, the Commission outlined a number of initiatives in the area of the retail financial services in response to the consultation on the Green Paper[31]. These initiatives included the publication of a White Paper on Mortgage Credit, which recognised the importance of the mortgage credit sector for consumers and the economy as a whole, as demonstrated by the sub-prime mortgage crisis in the United States.

Overview of Market Developments

125. In addition to the regulatory developments, a series of market developments have contributed to the integration of the EU financial services sector, including the ongoing consolidation of trading services in the EU, such as the Euronext/New York Stock Exchange merger; the OMX/Nasdaq merger and the London Stock Exchange/Borsa Italiana merger.

126. In the retail banking sector, there has been significant cross-border banking consolidation. Most recently, in the largest EU cross-border banking merger to date, a consortium of Royal Bank of Scotland, Fortis and Banco Santander acquired the Dutch bank ABN Amro.

127. In addition, a number of market-led reforms are due to be implemented to tackle fragmentation in the retail banking sector. The Single Euro Payments Area (SEPA) will include pan-European euro-denominated credit transfer and direct debit schemes and a pan-European framework for payment cards (applicable to all Member States including non-eurozone members). In particular, SEPA is designed to ensure that cross-border payments are as cheap and easy as domestic payments.

The Wholesale Sector

128. Integration has been achieved to a greater extent in the EU wholesale financial services sector. The Commission stated that this focus was intentionally adopted because a well-functioning wholesale sector was considered of strategic importance "as an engine for economic development" (Q 208).

129. Many witnesses concurred that, at this stage, "there is little need for more legislation in the wholesale area" (Barclays p 198). Rather, evidence was submitted that "at a time when the financial services industry is facing a period of enormous and costly institutional change as a result of the impact of the FSAP, it needs a substantial period to consolidate these changes effectively" (City of London Corporation p 213). This is, of course, only possible once all 42 FSAP measures are fully transposed into national law across the 27 Member States. Furthermore, some of the measures, notably

---

30 'Green Paper on Retail Financial Services in the Single Market', Commission, COM(2007)226.

31 'Initiatives in the area of retail financial services', Accompanying document to the Communication from the Commission to the European Parliament, the Council, the European Economic and Social Committee and the Committee of the Regions, SEC(2007) 1520.

the Markets in Financial Instruments Directive (MiFID), have only recently come into force[32].

130. Far from requiring new legislative proposals, it was suggested to us that the Commission should focus on implementation and on "ensuring that Member States are honouring their obligations equally" (APCIMS p 196). Evidence from British Bankers' Association (BBA), among others, indicated that implementation across the EU was patchy, especially with regard to MiFID (Q 117)[33]. However, despite concerns that only a few Member States would be in a position to meet the deadline for implementing MiFID, the Commission has recently announced that a majority of Member States have complied.[34]

131. A consistent theme was the failure of some Member States to implement EU directives in a timely and consistent manner, the effect of which is to undermine the impact of the initiatives and potentially to place those market participants in Member States who are compliant at a competitive disadvantage.

132. Although the Commission can initiate infringement proceedings against Member States under Article 226 of the EC Treaty, some witnesses felt that "Commission remedies are not always sufficient for enforcement" (Santander p 233). Other witnesses suggested that "The tools are available, but the Commission could devote more resource to studying the manner in which EU legislation has been implemented, and in its choice of the tools at its disposal" (Barclays p 201).

133. A number of witnesses, including APCIMS, suggested that "industry led solutions are in general far preferable to legislative initiatives where the outcomes can have unpredictable and unwanted conclusions" (p 197) and that the Commission should address any remaining barriers in this sector by using such solutions.

134. The EU Code for Clearing and Settlement may provide an example of self-regulation working successfully. On 7 November 2006, three main industry associations in the EU clearing and settlement sector signed the Code, which aimed at enhancing transparency and increasing competition in the post-trade EU clearing and settlement sector. The Code seeks to reduce the high cost of cross-border post-trade services in the EU. Following a Communication in 2004, the Commission mooted the need for a framework Directive imposing a range of obligations on the market, such as accounting separation and equal access. The Code was adopted by market participants in order to avoid the prospect of a directive. As the Code is currently being implemented by the market, it remains to be seen if it will lead to a reduction in the costs of cross-border clearing and settlement services in the EU[35]. If it

32 MiFID came into effect on 1 November 2007.

33 The Commission has already taken action against Member States for failing to take sufficient measures to implement MiFID (see Commission Press Release IP/07/547 'Commissioner McCreevy urges Member States to ensure rapid implementation of Markets in Financial Instruments Directive ("MiFID"), 24 April 2007); see also FSAP Evaluation: Part I: Process and Implementation', (Annex B), for details of transposition of FSAP directives as at 15 January 2007.

34 See Commission MEMO/07/439 'Markets in Financial Instruments Directive (MiFID): Frequently Asked Questions', 29 October 2007.

35 The Commission is expected to deliver a report to Ecofin in early 2008 on the Code's impact and enforceability.

does not then "the whole voluntary approach to reform will be open to doubt" (CBI p 219).

The Retail Sector

135. In contrast to the EU wholesale sector, there has been less integration of the EU retail banking sector. Witnesses largely attributed this to "different languages" (BBA Q 116) and "different consumer behaviour and legal frameworks" (Barclays p 198). We suspect that protectionism, at least in some Member States, also played a part.

136. The fragmented nature of the EU retail banking sector was also confirmed by the Commission's investigation into the EU retail banking sector which found that national competition barriers were widespread and that costs to companies and consumers were unnecessarily high. In addition to concluding that the sector was generally fragmented along national lines, the Commission also found a number of other factors (such as price rigidity and customer immobility) suggesting that competition in the EU retail banking market may not be working effectively.[36]

137. In terms of market-led developments, due to practical difficulties arising from organic growth (e.g. the establishment of branches in another Member State) or the provision of cross-border services (i.e. the bank and customer being located in different Member States), cross-border banking consolidation is expected to be the most effective means to integrate further the EU retail banking sector, subject to the principles of fair competition.[37]

138. As cross-border consolidation has, however, to date been driven by opportunities offered in specific markets, such as Banco Santander's purchase of Abbey, rather than by changes in EU legislation, some witnesses indicated that the Commission and, where applicable, NRAs should focus on "removing barriers which prevent or restrict market entry or the development of effective competition for retail products" (Barclays p 200).

139. The Commission has already taken some action to create such a level playing field. For example, in response to the resurgence of economic protectionism across the EU, as well as launching proceedings against a number of Member States,[38] the Commission has also revised the regulatory framework for the review of EU banking mergers to limit the discretion of NRAs. On 13 March 2007, the European Parliament and the Commission reached a compromise on a proposed directive limiting the duration of any review to 60 days and requiring NRAs to publish the grounds of any decision. It remains to be seen whether the directive will be sufficient to remove any hindrances to cross-border banking consolidation.

140. However, more needs to be done by the Commission to ensure that banks have equal access to other markets. There is particular support from market participants for the Commission's proposals in its final findings on the EU

---

36 See Commission Press Release IP/07/114 'Competition: Commission sector inquiry finds major barriers in retail banking', 31 January 2007.

37 See the UK response to the Green Paper on Retail Financial Services (paragraph 12).

38 See Commission Press Release IP/05/1595, 'Free movement of capital: Commission opens an infringement procedure against Italy in the issue of acquisition of stakes in domestic banks', 14 December 2005, and European Commission Press Release IP/06/227, 'Mergers: Commission launches procedure against Poland for preventing Unicredit/HVB merger', 8 March 2006.

sector inquiry and the White Paper on Mortgage Credit to provide increased access to credit databases.[39]

141. Although there is support for facilitating access to markets, some witnesses have urged the Commission to undertake thorough analysis before initiating any legislative proposals. In this respect, previous regulatory initiatives in the EU retail banking sector have been criticised for failing to assess benefits for consumers as part of the legislative process. The Consumer Credit Directive, for example, failed to "tackle key elements such as taxation, recovery process and protection of collateral harmonisation" that would have led to lower prices and higher quality of services and an "increase in cross-border activity" (Santander p 232). No impact assessment was undertaken as part of the regulatory process and a post-adoption study by the Commission has concluded that the Consumer Credit Directive will not achieve an internal market.[40]

142. Angela Knight suggested that "too often there is a leap to, 'What can we do? Where shall we do it? There must be this barrier or that barrier. Let's create a directive.'" (Q 118). Rather, consumer research should be carried out first. However, the regulatory approach alone is considered insufficient. Barclays stated that "We believe that a single market cannot be created through legislation alone and we welcome the increasing use of competition policy—and other non-legislative tools— ... as a means of opening markets" (p 199). This approach can be seen in enforcement actions against individual banks under Articles 81 or 82 of the EC Treaty and the review of financial services mergers falling within the scope of the EC Merger Regulation.

143. There are some signs that the Commission has listened to the calls from market participants. As part of the response to the consultation on the Green Paper on Retail Financial Services, the Commission has demonstrated a willingness to undertake further analysis and consultation before proposing any initiatives.[41] For example, the Commission recognised that further studies are needed in relation to product tying and the access to and availability of credit data. In addition, as advocated by the BBA, the Commission has encouraged a market-led solution in order to encourage switching between banks similar to the UK banking code.

Conclusions for Financial Services

144. Well-functioning financial markets play a significant role in delivering a range of benefits for individuals in the EU.[42] **At a macro-economic level, the Committee believes that completing the Single Market in financial services is a crucial part of the Commission's overriding objective of achieving more and better jobs in a more innovative and attractive Europe.** Deep, liquid, dynamic financial markets will also ensure the most efficient allocation and provision of capital and services throughout the

---

39 See, for example, the responses of Barclays, Royal Bank of Scotland and the British Bankers' Association to the Green Paper on Retail Financial Services.

40 See UK response to the Green Paper on Retail Financial Services.

41 'Initiatives in the area of retail financial services', Accompanying document to the Communication from the Commission to the European Parliament, the Council, the European Economic and Social Committee and the Committee of the Regions, SEC(2007) 1520.

42 See, for example, Green Paper on Financial Services Policy (2005–2010) (Annex I).

European economy. The Single Market in financial services is intended to provide increased competition and greater financial stability.

145. In addition, if investors can invest throughout the EU on the basis of clear and comparable information from securities issuers and without unnecessary red tape or additional costs compared to the cost of investing in their own Member State, then that investment is more likely to be allocated on the most efficient basis in terms of anticipated returns. In turn, if businesses have access to more abundant and cheaper capital, they can finance expansion more easily and produce their goods and services more efficiently, which ultimately means lower prices for consumers. Well-functioning markets will also optimise the value of savings and pensions for individuals.

146. Single Market measures to date have largely targeted the wholesale sector and there is, among market participants and stakeholders, a clear desire for a regulatory pause. Such a pause will allow the impact of the measures to date to be assessed. **The Commission should use such a pause to focus on its monitoring role and encourage the timely and consistent implementation of EU directives.**

147. Although integration in the EU retail banking sector is less advanced due to the characteristics of the sector, it is important for any initiatives to have a consumer-oriented approach in order to deliver tangible benefits to end-users by opening access to national markets. **As part of this approach, research and consultation must be the starting points before legislative proposals are launched.** The Commission has recognised that further studies and consultation should be undertaken before proposing any legislative proposals.

148. **Following such research and consultation the Commission should be more willing to develop a combination of market-led and regulatory instruments to be pursued in order to further the integration of the EU retail banking sector.**

CHAPTER 8: SUMMARY OF CONCLUSIONS AND RECOMMENDATIONS

149. We believe that the Single Market has the potential to be of great benefit to the businesses, citizens and consumers of the European Union. The Commission's Review of the Single Market is a useful and timely exercise to refocus policy on how to secure those benefits (paragraph 5).

150. We call on the Government and the Commission to instil a sense of urgency into the review of the Single Market (paragraph 59).

Policy-making and Implementation

151. The Committee strongly supports the Commission's commitment, made in the Single Market Review, to keep legislation simple, to roll back EU intervention where it is no longer appropriate, and to seek non-legislative solutions where possible (paragraph 60).

152. The Commission's Review rightly emphasises the importance of working in partnership with Member States and local authorities, but this Committee would place greater onus on the Member States to meet their commitments in order to achieve a fully-functioning Single Market (paragraph 61).

153. We believe effective policy-making underlies effective implementation. We welcome the Commission's proposals in its Review of the Single Market for better product and sector monitoring, consultation with a wider range of stakeholders and improved impact assessments (paragraph 62).

154. More effort and resources should be devoted to providing practical assistance to Member States in the process of transposing legislation in order to avoid problems of interpretation, delayed implementation or failure to enforce later on (paragraph 63).

155. The focus on assisting Member States early on in the process of transposition must not come at the expense of effective enforcement when necessary (paragraph 64).

156. We welcome the Commission's proposals for a more proactive approach to prevent problems in the implementation of EU law, promoting best practice through a Member State working group and supporting the exchange of information and staff between national administrations, as well as using competition powers, such as sector inquiries (paragraph 65).

Regulatory Authorities

157. National Regulatory Authorities must be independent of government, especially where governments have financial interests in the major market operator or national incumbent (paragraph 66).

158. There is no need for a 'super-regulator' at EU-level in any of the sectors we considered in this inquiry, which were energy, telecommunications and financial services (paragraph 67).

159. The Committee is pleased to see that the Commission's recent proposals suggest more cooperation between National Regulatory Authorities; the need for operational independence of regulators; and strengthened powers for regulators to ensure that consumers and businesses can reap the benefits of the Single Market (paragraph 68).

Realising the Benefits of the Single Market for Businesses, Citizens and Consumers

160. We believe that more should be done to help SMEs participate actively in the Single Market (paragraph 69).

161. Consumers and citizens need to be more fully persuaded of the benefits of the Single Market (paragraph 70).

162. We call for a renewed commitment to the importance of competition and the need to complete the Single Market for the benefit of consumers and businesses alike (paragraph 71).

Energy Sector

163. The practice of some network operators to discriminate against third parties in favour of their own related supply interests must be addressed. In this regard the Committee welcomes the Commission's legislative proposals (paragraph 95).

Energy Regulation

164. We are of the opinion that full ownership unbundling more satisfactorily removes the incentives for discriminatory and uncompetitive behaviour by the network operator (paragraph 96).

165. We support the creation of an agency for the cooperation of National Regulatory Authorities but would reject calls for a European regulatory authority (paragraph 97).

166. We accept that security of supply is important but we are not convinced that the creation of a more comprehensive Single Market in energy would necessarily weaken international supply (paragraph 98).

Telecommunications

Telecommunications Regulation

167. The main concern continues to be failures by Member States in the implementation and enforcement of certain elements of their regulatory obligations. The Commission has recognised this in its reform proposals, with new measures designed to improve its oversight of the decisions of Member State National Regulatory Authorities, to ensure greater consistency in approach between Member States. We therefore welcome its reform proposals in this respect (paragraph 115).

168. The Commission should consider what steps can be taken to reduce further the market power of the national incumbents. The Committee supports the Commission's proposal to enable National Regulatory Authorities to impose functional separation as a remedy (paragraph 116).

169. Despite the claims made by the Commission, the Committee believe that the creation of an EU regulator for the telecommunications sector is likely to increase regulatory complexity and uncertainty for market participants and bring insufficient benefits for the costs involved (paragraph 117).

Spectrum

170. We welcome the Commission's initiative on spectrum, including the facilitation of secondary trading; greater access to licence-free spectrum, and further co-ordination on the conditions applicable to spectrum authorisations (paragraph 118).

Financial Services

171. A desire for a regulatory pause in the wholesale banking sector was expressed. The Commission should use such a pause to focus on its monitoring role and encourage the timely and consistent implementation of EU directives (paragraph 146).

172. It is important for any retail banking sector initiatives to have a consumer-oriented approach in order to deliver tangible benefits to end-users by opening access to national markets. As part of this approach, research and consultation must be the starting points before legislative proposals are launched (paragraph 147).

173. Following such research and consultation the Commission should be more willing to develop a combination of market-led and regulatory instruments to be pursued in order to further the integration of the EU retail banking sector (paragraph 148).

APPENDIX 1: SUB-COMMITTEE B (INTERNAL MARKET)

The Members of the Sub-Committee which conducted this inquiry were:

Lord Bradshaw
Lord Dykes
Baroness Eccles of Moulton*
Lord Freeman (Chairman)
Lord Fyfe of Fairfield*
Lord Geddes*
Lord Haskel*
Lord James of Blackheath
Lord Lee of Trafford*
Lord Mitchell
Lord Paul
Lord Powell of Bayswater
Lord Rowe-Beddoe
Lord St John of Bletso*
Lord Walpole
Lord Whitty

* Former Members from the last session (2006–07), co-opted to complete the inquiry.

Declarations of Interests:

A full list of Members' interests can be found in the Register of Lords Interests:

http://www.publications.parliament.uk/pa/ld/ldreg.htm

Members declared no interests relevant to this inquiry.

APPENDIX 2: LIST OF WITNESSES

The following witnesses gave evidence. Those marked * gave oral evidence.

Association of Electricity Producers (AEP)

Association of Private Client Investment Managers and Stockbrokers (APCIMS)

Barclays

* British Bankers' Association (BBA)

* British Chambers of Commerce (BCC)

BT

* BusinessEurope

Business for New Europe

Centre for European Policy Studies

* Centrica Energy

Mr Giles Chichester MEP

City of London Corporation

Confederation of British Industry (CBI)

* Department for Trade and Industry (now the Department for Business, Enterprise and Regulatory Reform)

Engineering and Technology Board (ETB)

* European Commission

* European Consumers' Association (BEUC)

* European Economic and Social Committee, Single Market Observatory

* European Regulators' Group for Electricity and Gas (ERGEG)

* European Trade Union Confederation (ETUC)

* Federation of Small Businesses (FSB)

* Financial Services Authority (FSA)

* Gaz de France

* Global Vision

Mr Malcolm Harbour MEP

* HM Treasury

Mr Alan Littler

* Ms Arlene McCarthy MEP

* Mr Charlie McCreevy, Commissioner for Internal Market and Services

National Consumer Council (NCC)

* National Grid

* Ofcom

Office of Fair Trading (OFT)

* Ofgem
* Orange
* Portuguese Presidency of the Council
* POWEO
  Mr John Purvis MEP
  Santander
  Shell
* SOLVIT
* Mr Peter Sutherland
* Dr Mark Thatcher
  T-Mobile
* Mr Jacques Toubon MEP
  Vodafone
  Baroness Wilcox
* Lord Williamson of Horton

APPENDIX 3: CALL FOR EVIDENCE

1. The Internal Market Sub-Committee (Sub-Committee B) of the House of Lords Select Committee on the European Union is undertaking an inquiry into issues raised by the European Commission's Review of the Single Market.

2. On 10 May 2006 the Commission adopted a Communication "A Citizens' Agenda—delivering results for Europe". One of the major initiatives in the agenda is a fundamental and forward looking review of the EU Single Market. An interim report of the review was presented to the Spring European Council, and a final report is anticipated in Autumn 2007.

3. The Communication which launched this review called for the following four questions to be addressed:

- How can we build on what has already been achieved?
- Where are the remaining gaps?
- How can we meet the challenges of the future?
- Do we have the most effective mechanisms for delivering the Single Market?

4. The Sub-Committee's inquiry will take evidence from June 2007, and present a report in response to the publication of the findings of the Commission's review. As well as conducting an overview of the single market, the inquiry will focus on three key sectors:

- Energy markets;
- Financial services; and
- Telecommunications.

5. The Sub-Committee seeks evidence in particular in the following areas:

A. The Current State of the Single Market

- What has the impact of the recent enlargements of the European Union been on the single market?
- Are there significant barriers to firms seeking to offer their goods or services, or to consumers accessing these goods or services, in other Member States of the European Union? If so, what are the most important of those barriers? Are small businesses more likely to encounter barriers when seeking to offer their goods and services in other Member States? What measures are needed to overcome those barriers?
- Do you consider further legislative measures by the Commission to be necessary for the completion of the single market? If so, what measures would you consider appropriate?
- Are the current provisions for monitoring market functioning and performance effective? What evidence is there that Member States are honouring their obligations equally?
- Is there a need for greater cooperation between National Regulatory Authorities?

- Are the current remedies available to the Commission to enforce single market legislation adequate; and are they used effectively?
- What is your view of the Country of Origin Principle, whereby a company registered to provide services in one Member State is automatically qualified to provide those services in any other Member State on the basis of home country regulation? Does this Principle constitute the best basis for single market measures? How is cross-border activity by small businesses helped or hindered by the Country of Origin Principle?
- Do the concepts of the "national champion" and "economic nationalism" pose a threat to the single market?
- Should there be a greater role for technology and research in facilitating the single market?
- What is the significance of the single currency to the operation of the single market?

B. Sector-specific Questions

Energy

- Has there been sufficient unbundling of gas and electricity markets in all Member States?
- Is there agreement on the fundamental importance of a genuine single market to support a Common European strategy for energy?
- What are the implications for the single market of the Commission's commitments on climate change?
- Should there be a single EU energy regulator?

Telecommunications

- Is the EU telecommunications market genuinely cross-border at present?
- Is the current EU regulatory framework for telecommunications sufficiently technology neutral?
- Does this regulatory framework require modernisation?

Financial Services

- What has been the impact of the implementation of the Financial Services Action Plan as a whole; and in particular the Markets in Financial Instruments Directive?
- Do you support the Commission's Code of Conduct on Clearing and Settlement?

APPENDIX 4: BRIEFINGS ON THE SERVICES DIRECTIVE

The Department for Trade and Industry (now the Department for Business, Enterprise and Regulatory Reform)

Text used by the Services Team during an informal briefing for EU Sub-Committee B on 11 June 2007

The final text of the Directive was published in the Official Journal on 27 December 2006. At that point the three year countdown to implementation began.

As this Committee has already noted, implementation is a complex process. We will need the help and cooperation of all Whitehall Departments, local authorities and regulators, and must keep in close step with business, consumers and trade unions to ensure that we fully understand their requirements as consumers. Indeed we have established a regular meeting of key stakeholders from these groups to discuss implementation.

Essentially, there are 4 workstreams:

- Screening legislation and administrative practices to ensure that they comply with the Directive and amending and simplifying where necessary. We are carrying out an exercise with Other Government Departments to determine which pieces of legislation fall within the scope of the Directive. Legislation within scope is being assessed against a check list to see whether it complies with the Directive. Any provisions which are non-compliant will need to be amended or abolished as the case may be.

- Setting up a Point of Single Contact, a website through which service providers will be able to find out what they need to know about operating in the UK and complete the necessary formalities to do so. We have commissioned a short study to find out what potential users of the site want and expect from it. Provisional findings suggest, amongst other things, that the site needs to be proactive and integrate with existing business services and provide basic information free of charge. Once the study is finalised Ministers will be able to consider the findings along with the costs and practicalities before narrowing down the options.

- Setting up administrative cooperation arrangements between our competent authorities (supervisory or regulatory bodies such as professional bodies or local authorities) and those in other Member States. Competent authorities will be obliged to offer each other Mutual Assistance to enable the effective supervision of service providers. Mutual assistance requests will either be routed to competent authorities via National Liaison Points, or directly through the IMI (Internal Market Information) system currently being developed by the Commission. The IMI system will help authorities identify the correct corresponding authority in other Member States and will provide automatic translation of queries. The system is currently being piloted with the Mutual Recognition of Professional Qualifications Directive and once properly up and running we will be training our competent authorities in its use.

- Implementing the provisions in the Directive on quality of services, so that, for example, service recipients have access to some basic information on providers and can easily discover what the means of redress are in different Member States.

This is a major project by any standards. We have adopted project planning disciplines with clear milestones and deadlines and have identified key risks to ensure that we can implement on time and anticipate possible issues. We also have a Project Steering Board to advise us on implementation, comprising representatives of large and small businesses, consumers, those who will be involved in delivering the Directive, the Treasury and the Better Regulation Executive.

We intend to run a full public consultation on our plans, which we hope to launch in November. Following analysis of the responses, Ministers will need to take decisions on the policy issues and subsequently any amending legislation will need to be drafted and introduced. If any primary legislation is necessary, then work contributing to that Bill will have to be completed to meet fourth session deadlines.

Effective implementation is not just an internal matter. We also need to keep a close eye on and influence the implementation process in other Member States to ensure that the full benefits accrue to UK businesses and consumers. This is a strong message that we have been receiving from our business stakeholders in particular.

To this end, we have been participating actively in a series of implementation working groups organised by the Commission, sharing our views and ideas. Three have been held to date with more planned for the future. We have had bilateral discussions with the Commission and informal meetings with a wide range of Member States, both to discuss common points of interest and also to provide advice to those several Member States who have asked for it. In this way we can indirectly influence the implementation process across the EU.

We are also keen to provide opportunities for UK business groups and others to find out about implementation elsewhere. Today, Christian Storost from the Ministry responsible for implementing the Directive in Germany, has come to talk to a large gathering of our stakeholders and subsequently held discussions over lunch with a smaller group of business representatives.

That is a very brief summary of the current position. We would be happy to amplify these points in discussion or to try to answer any questions which you may have.

Letter dated 31 July 2007 from Mr Gareth Thomas MP to Lord Grenfell

Re: 15482/06—Services in the internal market

The Chairman of Sub-Committee B, Lord Freeman, wrote to my predecessor, the Rt Hon Ian McCartney MP, on 25 June 2007 following a meeting of Sub-committee B of the Select Committee on the European Union, which took place on 11 June. His letter discussed the implementation of the Services Directive and asked for additional information on the following points:

1. The Department's plans for the dissemination of information about the requirements for compliance with the Directive, in particular to small and medium-sized firms

We will be raising awareness of the Directive by:

- Publishing a consultation document setting out our proposals for implementation. This is planned for November this year.
- Updating information on the BERR website. Current information can be found at: http://www.berr.gov.uk/europeandtrade/europe/services-directive/page9583.html
- Continuing our regular e-bulletin alerting stakeholders to developments. There are currently over a thousand subscribers.
- Holding meetings and events for stakeholders. For example we held an event on 11 June attended by over 100 stakeholders. This particular event included presentations by officials from both BERR and the German Federal Government implementation teams, as well as from Panlogic Ltd, who undertook a survey for us on likely user requirements for the Points of Single Contact. We also undertake presentations and briefings for individual organisations when asked.
- Regular meetings with a core group of key stakeholders representing all sizes of business, consumer groups and the unions and including the CBI, BCC, IoD and FSB. These organisations in their turn disseminate information to their members.
- Writing articles to appear in stakeholders' journals, magazines and newsletters where appropriate.
- Our policy concerning the implementation of any obligations on service providers under the Directive (for example, the information obligations in Article 22) will be formulated through consultation with stakeholders. Information on any such obligations developed will be disseminated through the routes set out above.

2. The tools available to the European Commission to police the Directive

The European Commission is organising regular meetings with Member States in order to encourage effective and consistent implementation, for example through the sharing of best practice, and it will be issuing Member States with guidance on implementation later this summer. Immediately after the deadline for implementation, Member States will commence a six-month peer-review of other Member States' compliance with the Directive based on their submitted implementation reports. BERR is working with the Commission and other Member States to ensure that this process is as robust and transparent as possible. Additionally, once the deadline has passed, the Commission will be able to commence infraction proceedings against any Member State that has not implemented the Directive properly.

3. Services omitted from the Directive and which would benefit from inclusion in the future

A broad summary of some of the sectors excluded from the Directive is set out below. The detail of these provisions is in Articles 1 to 3.

Sectors and groupings excluded from the scope of the Directive:

Non-economic services of general interest (SGIs)

Financial services

Electronic communications

Transport services

Temporary work agencies

Healthcare

Audio visual

Gambling

Exercise of official authority

Certain social services

Private security services

Notaries and bailiffs

Taxation

Article 17 also sets out a long list of sectors and groupings derogated from the provisions concerning the Freedom to Provide Services.

Some areas unaffected by the Directive are criminal law, labour law and private international law.

The Sub-Committee will recall the controversial history of this Directive and that negotiations were protracted. The final text represents a good outcome for the UK and our priority now is to ensure that the Directive is implemented effectively and on time across the EU. Some areas that are excluded from the scope of the Directive or derogated from the freedom to provide services provisions are covered by other EU internal market directives. However, the Government considers that further measures are needed in some of these key sectors such as energy, telecoms, financial services and postal services. Key barriers include continued existence of protected national monopolies, as well as legislative requirements and burdensome administrative practices.

I hope that you and the Chairman of Sub-Committee B will find this information useful.

Clifford Chance

Text used by Clifford Chance during an informal briefing for EU Sub-Committee B on 11 June 2007

1. What is the implementation Deadline?

Member States have until 28 December 2009 to ensure all elements of the Directive are implemented.

2. What are the "four pillars" of the Directive?

- **ART. 9–13 screening**—ensure all legislations/licences and administrative practices relating to service providers comply with the Directive, meaning remove or amend any laws and practices which create unjustifiable barriers to trade. ART 14, 20—prohibition; ART 15—evaluation

- **ART 6–8 point of single contact**—setting up an online portal through which businesses will be able to complete the formalities and procedures needed to set up a business or provide a service on a temporary basis

- **ART 28–29 mutual assistance**—Regulators will be enabled to co-operate more efficiently with their counterparts in other Member States.

- **ART 26 Quality of services**—the Directive also includes provisions on rights for service recipients, such as making information on redress schemes more readily available.

3. Role of the Commission, Parliament and Council

In addition, each Member State is required to report back to the Commission on what legislation and practices they have retained and the justification.

The Commission have planned to hold several Working Groups during the course of the implementation stages with Member States, to discuss aspects of the Directive and share best practice. The UK will be playing an active role in these.

On 4 June 2007 the Commission invited national and European professional associations and their members to provide information on existing and planned codes of conduct.

The Parliament will host an open hearing on implementation in mid-2008

The Commission is to report to Parliament on the application of the Directive at the end of the implementation period and every three years thereafter (ART 41)

4. Consequences of non-implementation

After the implementation date (28 December 2009) the Directive will have direct effect against a Member State.

This means that its provisions can be invoked by individuals provided those provisions are (i) clear, precise and unconditional and (ii) not dependent on further implementation by the Member State

A directive does not generally create rights and obligations between individuals. HOWEVER,

- UK Courts will have an obligation to interpret UK legislation in the light of the Directive; and
- UK Courts have a duty to cooperate.

5. What measures can a UK service provider take if he encounters legal obstacles in other Member States which are not compatible with the Directive

Option 1: Complain to the European Commission

Option 2: Complain to the DTI

Option 3: Go ahead and ignore the legal requirement

6. What sanctions are available against a Member State that fails to implement

Option 1: The UK could take another Member State to Court

Option 2: The European Commission could take another Member State to Court

Option 3: The service provider could claim damages against the Member State in question

Additional information submitted to Sub-Committee B by Clifford Chance

Background

On 19 January 2004, the European Commission (the Commission) published a draft Directive aimed at creating a single market in services industries. The proposal faced significant political opposition and was subject to significant amendments by the European Parliament (the Parliament).

In 2005, the Internal Market Sub-Committee B of the House of Lords Select Committee on the European Union (the Committee) conducted an inquiry on the proposal and considered the criticisms in its report "*Completing the Internal Market in Services*".[43] The Committee concluded that the proposal did not pose a threat to the health and safety of employees or consumers, nor did it pose a threat to consumer protection or environmental standards. It also concluded that services of general economic interest should not be excluded from the Directive. According to the Committee, many of the arguments raised against the proposal appeared to be either based upon misunderstandings or were seeking to obstruct change and the effective operation of the free movement of services in the European Union (EU).

On 5 April 2006, the Commission published an amended draft of the Directive, in which it largely incorporated changes made by the Parliament to the original proposal. For instance, the "country of origin principle" was removed from the text of the new draft in favour of a "freedom to provide services".

On 24 July 2006, the Committee conducted a follow-up inquiry and published a report, "*The Services Directive Revisited*", which compared the Commission's revised draft Directive to the original proposal in the light of the findings of their previous report.[44] While the Committee concluded that the revised draft Directive should be supported, it expressed concerns that the DTI may be underestimating some of the potential problems in implementing the legislative and registrative changes in the UK.[45]

The Directive was finally adopted at the Transport, Telecommunications & Energy Council on 11 December 2006 and thereafter published in the Commission's Official Journal on 27 December 2006.

Summary of previous oral evidence given to the Committee by Oliver Bretz and John Osborne

Country of Origin Principle

The Country of Origin Principle is a fundamental principle recognised under settled case law of the European Court of Justice (ECJ) and can still be invoked regardless of the precise wording of the Directive. In the absence of any harmonisation in the field of services across the EU, a restriction can only be based on rules justified by overriding requirements relating to the public interest and applicable to all persons and undertakings operating in the territory of the Member State where the service is provided, but only insofar as that interest is not safeguarded by the rules to which the provider of such a service is subject in his home Member State.

---

43 European Union Committee, 5th Report (2005-06): *Completing the internal market in services* (HL 23)

44 European Union Committee, 38th Report (2005-06): *The Services Directive Revisited* (HL 215)

45 *Ibid.* page 26.

The Directive is still a useful legal instrument because it will offer those service providers who operate across national boundaries on a temporary basis far greater confidence than would otherwise exist through the case-by-case application of the rules and general criteria established in the case law of the ECJ. Although its provisions do no more than reflect the case law, following the expiry of the deadline to transpose the Directive they will have direct effect in national laws and make it considerably easier for individuals who wish to provide services cross-borders to allege a breach of their freedom to do so. The Directive almost switches the burden to the Member States by forcing them to adopt certain measures into national law. If a Member State fails to do so, the individuals concerned can rely upon the provisions of the Directive against the Member State in question. In this respect, the Directive will be effective because specific articles can be invoked as opposed to general principles set out by the Community courts, which by their nature are much more difficult to interpret and much more open to debate. In addition, the Directive encourages service providers to go cross-border by amongst other measures requiring Member States to set up single points of contact.

Temporary nature of services v Established nature of services

The ECJ has consistently held that the temporary nature of an activity should be determined in the light not only of the duration of the provision of the service, but also of its regularity, periodical nature or continuity. This settled-case law has rendered the notion of services on a "temporary provision" very difficult to define in a meaningful manner. The meaning of "temporary provision" may vary depending upon the specific activity and how it is actually delivered on a cross-border basis. Under the Directive, which does not provide a definition of "temporary" in Article 4, as long as the services are not being provided on an indefinite basis, it can be interpreted that they will be provided on a temporary capacity.

The Directive has instead focused on the notion of establishment. A business established in one Member State could provide services and have infrastructure in another Member State without being established in that Member State (free movement of services).[46] Alternatively, a business could form a second establishment and therefore become subject to the same conditions as the nationals of that Member State (freedom of establishment).

Mutual recognition of professional qualifications

The Directive on the recognition of professional qualifications applies a Country of Origin Principle to professional qualifications.[47] It is a major door-opening exercise to provide services in Member States where there are very high barriers to entry in terms of qualification.

Posting of Workers Directive

Where service providers post workers to another Member State their main employment conditions will be governed by the rules of the host Member State, which remains entirely competent to define who qualifies as a worker (and who is to be regarded as a "false independent").

---

46 Establishment is "the actual pursuit of an economic activity through a fixed establishment of a provider for an indefinite period" (Article 4 of the Directive).

47 Directive 2005/36/EC of the European Parliament and of the Council on the recognition of professional qualifications (Official Journal L255 of 30 September 2005.

Legal obligations to change legislation arising under the provisions set out in the directive

Services Directive Requirements	UK Implementation	Commission cooperation
Scope		
Services of general economic interest (Art. 1.3.2)	What would the definition cover under UK law (regulated professions, business services, and distributive trade)?	Communication from the Commission on services of general interest in Europe (2001/C 17/04)
	How should they be organised and financed?	
Access to a service activity		
Authorisation schemes (Art. 9–13)	What services will require authorisation for reasons of public policy, public security, public health or the protection of the environment?	
	What administrative procedures and formalities will be required for granting authorisation (licences, approvals or concessions)? Would interviews be required (Recital 53)?	
	What will be the established selection procedures where the number of authorisations for a given activity is limited?	
Points of single contact (PSC) (Art. 6–8)	What facilities the PSC will require (electronic procedures)?	
	What information will be easily accessible to providers and recipients?	
	How will the PSC communicate/interact with competent authorities?	
Exercise of a service activity		
Multidisciplinary activities (Art. 25)		
Quality of services (Art. 26)	What will the UK require in terms of information & transparency?	On-going consultation on codes of conduct
Mutual assistance—Enforcement and	How many UK liaison points will be involved? (Art. 28.2)	Internal market information (IMI)[48]:

Regulatory Cooperation (Art. 28 & 29)	Where will the UK liaison point be located? Supervision procedures—factual checks and controls (Art. 28.4)	requests for information; checks; inspections or investigations
Alert mechanism (Art. 32)		IMI The Commission can consider publishing a communication similar to the Communication from the Commission to the Council and the European Parliament—Civil protection—State of preventive alert against possible emergencies (COM/2001/0707 final)

Implementation process

The UK is required to give effect to the Directive in its national law preferably before 28 December 2008 and no later than 28 December 2009.[49] A period of two years is proposed for implementation of laws, regulations and administrative provisions necessary to comply with the Directive. A period of a further year is allowed for the Commission's evaluation of reports on the implementation supplied by Member States.

What will be the involvement of the EU institutions in the implementation process?

European Commission

Since early 2007, the Commission has been hosting and coordinating working group meetings with the Member States on different implementation issues.

Implementation is also monitored and reviewed yearly by the Heads of State and Government at the EU Spring Summit Meetings (European Council).[50]

On 4 June 2007, the Commission invited national and European professional associations and their members to provide information on their existing and planned codes of conduct and to give their opinions on how best to develop codes of conduct at European level.

By 28 December 2008, the UK (and other Member States) will be required to report back to the Commission on what legislation and practices it has retained and the justifications.

Following the expiry on 28 December 2009 of the deadline to transpose the Directive and by 28 December 2011 and every three years thereafter, the

---

48 IMI will also include computer applications specific to a particular area such as Electronic Commerce or Professional Qualifications.

49 Article 44 of the Directive.

50 The last EU Spring Summit Meeting took place in Brussels on 8 and 9 March 2007.

Commission will be required to report to the Parliament on the application of the Directive, accompanied where appropriate by proposals for additional initiatives.[51]

European Parliament and Council of Ministers

The Parliament will be hosting an open hearing on the Directive's implementation in mid-2008.

How will the UK proceed with implementation?

Screening and initial proposals

The Department of Trade and Industry (the DTI) is the UK government department responsible for implementation of the Directive. The DTI has set up a Services Team to coordinate a thorough and careful review of existing UK relevant legislation regarding the supply of services to ensure that it complies with the market-opening criteria in the Directive. The Services Team is working to identify (i) any provisions of the Directive that have already been given effect in the UK by existing legislation and other rules as well as any provisions which would have to be repealed or amended in order to comply with the principles set out in the Directive; (ii) set out rules on regulatory and administrative requirements concerning access to and the exercise of a service activity; (iii) determine those specific requirements that are subject to an absolute prohibition in the proposed Directive (e.g., under Articles 14, 20) and those which are subject to evaluation (e.g., under Article 15). The Services Team is also working on two other main strands to implementation, namely the establishments of points of single contact and liaison points for mutual assistance.

The requirements of the Directive are complex and implementation will require the involvement and co-operation of a number of other government departments and public bodies. An interdepartmental group may be required to examine the draft legislation and identify any difficulties regarding land-use planning obligations and the identification of a competent authority.

Public consultation

The DTI will publish an implementation plan, the Services Directive implementation project, providing a comprehensive update on how it also intends to approach implementation of the Directive in the UK. This plan should explain the policy reasons behind the proposed implementation.

Stakeholders should be invited to comment on the benefits and the costs, which they consider, may be derived from the proposed implementation plan and be kept up to date with this work.

In the autumn of 2007, the DTI will run a three-month formal public consultation on the proposed legislative changes necessary to implement the Directive and publish a feedback statement on responses to the consultation on the DTI's website when the rest of the implementing regulations are laid.

Revision of the proposals

The DTI will revise its proposals in the light of responses to the consultation.

The Better Regulation Executive in the Cabinet Office should scrutinise DTI's own proposals to identify any instances of over-implementation.

---

[51] Article 41 of the Directive.

The DTI will lay down before Parliament new laws in the form of a bill if primary legislation is required or in the alternative it may proceed by way of statutory instruments (orders, rules or regulations).[52] Explanatory memorandums will be required to explain the key changes the statutory instruments will make to existing legislation. In addition, impact assessments will be carried out in order to enable the Government to weigh up and present the relevant evidence.[53]

52 Statutory Instruments are a form of legislation, which allows the provisions of an Act of Parliament to be subsequently brought into force, or altered without Parliament having to pass a new Act. They are also referred to as secondary, delegated or subordinate legislation.

53 Impact assessments were previously known as the Regulatory Impact Assessment.

APPENDIX 5: RECENT REPORTS

Recent Reports from the Select Committee

Session 2006–07

Correspondence with Ministers January–September 2006 (40th Report, HL Paper 187)

Remaining Government Responses Session 2004–05, Government Responses Session 2005–06 (37th Report, HL Paper 182)

Annual Report 2007 (36th Report, HL Paper 181)

EU Reform Treaty: work in progress (35th Report, HL Paper 180)

Evidence from the Minister for Europe on the June European Union Council and the 2007 Inter-Governmental Conference (28th Report, HL Paper 142)

The Further Enlargement of the EU: follow-up Report (24th Report, HL Paper 125)

The Commission's Annual Policy Strategy for 2008 (23rd Report, HL Paper 123)

Evidence from the Ambassador of the Federal Republic of Germany on the German Presidency (10th Report, HL Paper 56)

The Commission's 2007 Legislative and Work Programme (7th Report, HL Paper 42)

Government Responses: Session 2004–05 (6th Report, HL Paper 38)

Evidence from the Minister for Europe on the Outcome of the December European Council (4th Report, HL Paper 31)

Reports Prepared by Sub-Committee B (Internal Market)

Session 2006–07

Mobile Phone Charges in the EU: Curbing the Excesses (17th Report, HL Paper 79)

Television Without Frontiers? (3rd Report, HL Paper 27)

Session 2005–2006

Inquiry into the European Commission's Green Paper, "A European Strategy for Sustainable, Competitive and Secure Energy" (41st Report, HL Paper 224)

The Services Directive Revisited (38th Report, HL Paper 215)

Seventh Framework Programme for Research (33rd Report, HL Paper 182)

Including the Aviation Sector in the European Union Emissions Trading Scheme (21st Report, HL Paper 107)

Completing the Internal Market in Services (6th Report, HL Paper 23)

Printed in the United Kingdom by The Stationery Office Limited
2/2008 390640 19585

ISBN 978-0-10-401224-6